Harper Collins 25556 £9-90

D0415611

Supporting Children with
Dyslexia

Hull Learning Services

David Fulton Publishers

David Fulton Publishers Ltd
The Chiswick Centre, 414 Chiswick High Road, London W4 5TF

David Fulton Publishers is a division of Granada Learning, part of ITV plc.

www.fultonpublishers.co.uk

First published in Great Britain by David Fulton Publishers 2004

10 9 8 7 6 5 4 3 2 1

Note: The right of the authors to be identified as the authors of this work has been asserted by them in accordance with the Copyright, Designs and Patents Act 1988.

British Library Cataloguing in Publication Data
A catalogue record for this book is available from the British Library.

ISBN 1 84312 222 7

Typeset by Matrix Creative, Wokingham
Printed and bound in Great Britain

Contents

Appendices:

Foreword

This book was written and compiled by:

> Carol McGill M.Ed., Dip.Ed. (Specific Learning Difficulties), Dip.Ed. (Special Educational Needs), Kingston upon Hull SEN Support Service

in partnership with:

> Bernard Levey, Principal Educational Psychologist BSc, MSc, Kingston upon Hull City Psychological Service

with thanks to senior adviser John Hill for his support and encouragement throughout the development of this series. It is one of a series of eleven titles providing an up-to-date overview of special educational needs for Special Educational Needs Co-ordinators (SENCOs), teachers and other professionals, and parents.

The books were produced in response to training and information needs raised by teachers, support staff and parents in Hull. The aim of these books is to raise awareness and address many of the issues involved in creating inclusive environments.

For details of other titles and how to order, please go to: www.fultonpublishers.co.uk, or telephone 0500 618052.

Introduction

Dyslexia is a recognised condition which continues to be the subject of debate. In itself the word DYSLEXIA is from the Greek dys- meaning 'difficult', lexia to do with language. Similar difficulties such as dyspraxia are derived from 'difficult', with praxia referring to the learned ability to carry out a series of co-ordinated movements; while dyscalculia refers to 'difficulties' in calculia or abilities to calculate number. Dyslexia is often also referred to as a specific learning difficulty (Spld) in relation to literacy.

If assessed to be severe it can fall under the Disability Discrimination Act (1995), amended by the SEN and Disability Act (2001) (SENDA). This can benefit students and those who wish to go into Higher Education, because assessment can also aid and support exam conditions.

As part of the inclusion agenda, most pupils with dyslexia are educated within mainstream schools. In the post-16 sector there is a growing understanding of the needs dyslexic students have for ongoing support and their needs within the workplace. Many pupils may show elements or characteristics of dyslexia. However, it is the degree or severity of these characteristics that will affect pupils long term. The strategies and thinking identified within this book should benefit all pupils.

Many of the practices built up within schools which follow current thinking and good practice can support dyslexic pupils. As per the SEN Code of Practice schools should try their best to develop a dyslexic-friendly culture, which will also support the majority of other pupils.

Guidance can be provided by psychologists, Special Educational Needs Support Services and specially trained teachers from the public or private sector.

Guidance here aims at providing information to support the understanding and the teaching of the pupil with dyslexia. It is not definitive or hierarchical but a starting point on which to build, and may be 'dipped into' as your needs and circumstances demand.

What is dyslexia?

There are many definitions of dyslexia. Degrees of differences exist between authorities who study dyslexia and it continues to be the subject of research. Some definitions are given below:

> *"Dyslexia is present when the authorisation of word identification (reading) and/or word spelling does not develop or does so very incompletely or with great difficulty."*
>
> Health Council of the Netherlands 1997

> *"Dyslexia is evident when accurate and fluent word reading and/or spelling develops very incompletely or with great difficulty. This focuses on literacy learning at 'word level' and implies that the problem is severe and persistent despite appropriate learning opportunities. It provides the basis for a staged process of assessment through teaching."*
>
> British Psychological Society 1999
> (Dyslexia, Literacy and Psychological Assessment)

> *"Dyslexia causes difficulties in learning to read, write and spell. Short-term memory, mathematics, concentration, personal organisation and sequencing may also be affected.*
>
> *Dyslexia usually arises from a weakness in the processing of language-based information. Biological in origin, it tends to run in families, but environmental factors also contribute.*
>
> *Dyslexia can occur at any level of intellectual ability. It is not the result of poor motivation, emotional disturbance, sensory impairment or lack of opportunities, but it may occur alongside any of these.*
>
> *The effects of dyslexia can be largely overcome by skilled specialist teaching and the use of compensatory strategies."*
>
> Dyslexia Institute September 2002

The DfES does not give a definition but identifies dyslexia as:

> *"a condition that affects the ability to process language. Dyslexic learners often have difficulties in the acquisition of literacy skills and in some cases the problems will manifest themselves into mathematics… This pattern of abilities and weaknesses is known as 'specific learning difficulties'."*

The DfES links dyslexia and dyscalculia within its document on guidance and support in daily maths lessons. It identifies that:

"Dyscalculia is a condition that affects the ability to acquire arithmetical skills… Very little is known about the prevalence of dyscalculia, its causes, or treatments …It is more likely that difficulties with numeracy accompany the language difficulties of dyslexia."

Dyscalculia (difficulties within maths) (Sharma 1990) is a growing area of research, with an estimated 6 per cent of all children showing signs of developmental dyscalculia (www.dyscalculia.org/edu503html).

Dyslexia itself can be subdivided into:

- Developmental dyslexia – something you are born with.
- Acquired dyslexia – following an injury to the brain, e.g. via an accident or stroke.

Dyslexia and disability

- Dyslexia is covered by the Disability Discrimination Act (1995).
- Students in Higher Education who have been formally assessed as dyslexic can apply to the LEA for a Disabled Students' Allowance.
- Consideration of the SEN and Disability Act (2001) (SENDA) and the Human Rights Act (2000) in relation to dyslexia can have legal implications. Legal and operational perspectives can be seen in Appendix 7.

What is developmental dyslexia?

There have been many definitions of childhood developmental dyslexia, some of which have defined dyslexia as the inability to acquire literacy despite normal intelligence. Other definitions have described dyslexia in terms of a list of presenting symptoms (e.g. left/right confusion, poor recall of a string of digits) and still others have described dyslexia as simply the inability to learn to read or write.

It is fortunate and timely that there has now developed a growing consensus about a definition of dyslexia among psychologists and researchers. The consensus view is best represented by the definition of dyslexia provided by a working party set up by the British Psychological Society (BPS), which reported in 1999. The **working definition** of dyslexia produced by this party is as follows:

> *"Dyslexia is evident when accurate and fluent word reading and/or spelling develops very incompletely or with great difficulty. This focuses on literacy learning at the 'word level' and implies that the problem is severe and persistent despite appropriate learning opportunities. It provides the basis for a staged process of assessment through teaching."*

The implications of this definition for teachers and other professionals working with children who have literacy difficulties are as follows:

1. For a child to be described as dyslexic he/she has to have had *severe and persistent* problems in learning to read and spell. A child who has severe and persistent problems may also have other types of symptoms (e.g. laterality problems, poor short-term memory, poor personal organisation skills), *but* of themselves, these are insufficient if a child is to be described as dyslexic, unless the child concerned has severe and persistent literacy difficulties in learning to read or spell at the *word level*.

2. The definition restricts the use of the term dyslexia to children who have a word decoding and spelling (encoding) problem. Children who can read mechanically (fluently bark at print) but do not understand what they read are not dyslexic but hyperlexic (see Figure 1). The problems of this latter group are nonetheless of legitimate concern to teachers, since the whole purpose of teaching children to decode words is to help them access and understand information through print. However, hyperlexics require remedial programmes that focus on comprehension, not decoding.

	Meaning	
Independent reader Poor speller High interest (improved dyslexic pupil)		Good reader Good speller High interest (good reader)
		Print
Can't read Can't spell Not interested (stuck dyslexic pupil)		Mechanical reader Good speller Poor comprehension (hyperlexic)

Figure 1 Differences between the dyslexic pupil and the hyperlexic pupil

3. The definition makes no mention of intelligence and this is because it is the consensus view that dyslexia is no respecter of intelligence and occurs in children of all abilities. In short, the term dyslexia is no longer reserved for children who are poor readers but of average or above average intelligence. This latter group of children are dyslexic but their dyslexia is a **specific literacy difficulty** (Spld) the context of overall average ability.

    It should come as no surprise that dyslexia can occur in children of all abilities since other conditions such as autism, attention deficit disorder (ADD) and dyspraxia also occur across the ability range.

    However, although the term dyslexia can be applied to children of all ability levels, it is simply not sensible to use the term in the case of children who have extremely severe learning difficulties.

4. The definition does not rule out the possibility of the early identification of dyslexia before a child reaches school age and is taught to read. It is well established that children who have difficulties in language acquisition are more likely to have reading problems. Educators in the pre-school phase will be alert to the needs of children with language difficulties and equally, through assessment based on the Foundation Curriculum, they will assess children and identify their learning needs across all areas of their development. Early identification will lead to early intervention and thus reduce the likelihood of later educational failure, including reading failure.

5. The definition calls for a staged process of *assessment* through teaching by teachers and other educators. It follows, and is implicit in this working definition, that an ongoing evaluation of a child's responses to the teaching of reading and spelling is a legitimate form of assessment and will inform later interventions. The teacher is, therefore, central to the process of defining a child's difficulties and needs. One-off assessments such as those conducted by specialist teachers or psychologists have a place in profiling a child's cognitive strengths and weaknesses, but these cannot replace ongoing teacher assessment of a child's acquisition of literacy skills.

6. The definition stresses the importance of the teaching of literacy and *providing appropriate learning strategies*. The presence of severe and persistent difficulties in word decoding and spelling does not imply that remediation is pointless. Although dyslexia is a 'disability' (SENDA 2001), its effects (i.e. impoverished literacy skills) can be ameliorated by appropriate instruction which is pitched at the right level, is motivating, boosts confidence and which gives the child self-respect.

7. The definition states that for a child to be described as having dyslexia, the problems at the word decoding and encoding levels must be severe and persistent. The degree of severity and persistency is not defined. Therefore, by implication, the level of severity and persistency must lie on a continuum, ranging from extreme to moderate dyslexia. Thus, a few pupils with dyslexia may never progress beyond sight word recognition. Others with a less extreme form of the disability learn to read, but continue to have major spelling difficulties. Still others, who have overcome the most disabling features of dyslexia, continue to have problems in reading and writing at speed, sentence structure and maintenance of attention when reading. The fact that dyslexia lies on a continuum mirrors other disabilities (e.g. childhood autism), but the definition rules out reading difficulties that are not severe or persistent.

Facts about dyslexia

- Dyslexia may occur in children of *all* abilities.

- Within the dyslexia profile individuals can show different strengths and weaknesses.

- Difficulties can be slight, moderate or severe.

- Dyslexia occurs in both males and females but is far more common in males.

- Research suggests that 4–5% of all ability children may be severe dyslexics; 10% are affected at different levels and in different ways.

- Dyslexia is a disability individuals will have for life.

- In understanding its characteristics, strategies and approaches can be introduced to support learning, enabling individuals to reach their potential, maintain their self-esteem and motivation, and to develop their strengths. The earlier the recognition and interaction, the less chance there is of frustration and failure developing.

- Dyslexic pupils who are nurtured can display strengths of ingenuity, creativity and lateral thinking. They are likely to have good spatial and/or verbal skills, contribute well in discussions, solve puzzles and be good at design, building and construction.

- There may be overlapping characteristics between other specific learning difficulties such as dyspraxia, attention deficit hyperactivity disorder (ADHD) and syndromes on a similar continuum. Appendices 1 and 2 identify similarities and contrasts between dyslexia and dyspraxia.

- Several genes have been identified as possible causative factors. If one parent is dyslexic there is a 50% chance that any of his/her children will inherit dyslexia.

- Brain imaging has shown differences in specific areas of the dyslexic brain compared to non-dyslexic brains.

Causal elements of dyslexia

Simply, the causal elements of dyslexia appear to be biological in nature affecting, in varying degrees, some cognitive functions. These can be seen as observable behaviours affecting learning outcomes.

> Biological elements

- Dyslexia can be **genetic**, running in families (checking the family history can be useful).

- There can be **imbalances and interaction** between the right and left sides of the brain:
    - right side: supporting creative, spatial and visual areas;
    - left side: supporting language, logic and sequence.

- There can be **cerebellar developmental delay**.

> Cognitive difficulties

- **Short-term working memory**
    - Problems arise within auditory and/or visual recall.
    - Processing of information is slow, resulting in lost information.
    - Overload on the 'memory shelf' can result in old or new information not being stored or acquired.

- **Phonological processing**
  Problems arise in processing sounds and some types of language skills.

- **Synthesising information**
  Problems arise in bringing all the information stored in the brain together. There may also be elements of 'perception' where auditory and/or visual information is not processed completely, accurately or efficiently.

- **Sequencing**
  Problems occur in the areas of order and sequence, e.g.:
    - time sequences
    - number sequences
    - gross/fine motor sequences (co-ordination)
    - alphabet (letter order)

Identification

The elements of biological and cognitive difficulties previously outlined are reflected in observable characteristics or behaviours which may help in the identification of dyslexia.

Difficulties can arise from any identification by non-specialists as many of the observed behaviours can have similar characteristics to different syndromes (e.g. between dyslexia and dyspraxia; see Appendices 1 and 2). Difficulties may also be the result of developmental delay or health problems affecting ears/and or eyes at an important developmental stage, causing difficulties in phonological acquisition and/or reading problems. Absences from school can also affect learning at Key Stages and this needs to be considered when looking at the difficulties the particular pupil may have in acquiring skills.

There will also be a difference between a mildly dyslexic pupil and a moderate or severe dyslexic pupil. Profiles of strengths and weaknesses can also vary. At any level of dyslexia a pupil may exhibit a different number of characteristics in different areas. These will affect learning, and often behavioural and emotional responses.

Concerns as to pupil progress, especially within literacy, may be observed by both parents and teachers. Observation of difficulties, strengths and weaknesses can build an assessment picture. Other areas that can be helpful when building up a picture of a pupil with specific difficulties are:

- family background (especially fathers, brothers, uncles, grandfathers with literacy problems);
- birth knowledge (difficulties, length of time in labour);
- developmental history (the age and school stage of the pupil);
- age, stage and working levels (National Curriculum) as against teacher assessment and observations.

The various types of support implemented within the school should be recorded together with the outcomes. More formal assessments, reading comprehension, spelling tests along with working, and SATs levels can be made by the school. More formal, detailed assessments can be made by specifically trained staff, often found in support services. Fuller assessments can be made by educational psychologists.

The following pages look at the observed behaviours of:

- **Foundation Stage pupils** • **Primary pupils** • **Secondary pupils**

who may exhibit a variety of dyslexic characteristics. These characteristics will be evident throughout a pupil's school career, but will be more evident at different stages and in different learning contexts.

Appendix 4 provides examples of assessments which may be used across age ranges. These need to be done with understanding and knowledge.

Identification in the Foundation Stage

Aspects for identification

Foundation Stage teachers may identify strengths and weaknesses from observations and assessments via the Foundation Stage Profile which will indicate concern.

Strengths may be seen in play:

- in building and construction activities;
- in geometric and pattern activities;
- in problem-solving activities.

Weaknesses

Memory:

- remembering auditory and visual information;
- recalling a sequenced activity;
- forgetting instructions.

Sequencing:

- action songs;
- nursery rhymes;
- numbers;
- threading beads to a pattern;
- handwriting and letter/number formation;
- dressing.

Speech:

- muddled and jumbled words and letters, e.g. 'par cark' (car park);
- problems in recalling names (people and objects);
- problems in word finding and/or categorisation, e.g. can't recall the name for a chair but remembers it's a piece of furniture, or remembers 'animal' but forgets 'dog';
- problems processing sounds and linking to a letter shape;
- slow speech development.

Language:

- processing and responding to spoken or written language;
- following instructions;
- retelling a simple story;
- enjoyment in listening to stories but not interested in learning to read (words, letters, books);
- problems using the correct words.

Listening:

- poor concentration;
- difficulties in discriminating between similar words and letters (dog/god), (van/fan), (v/th/f);
- difficulties identifying rhyme and rhythm.

Motor skills:

- either/both fine/gross motor skills;
- movement and balance;
- throwing, kicking and catching (ball skills generally);
- running and skipping;
- difficulties with left/right, shoes/gloves;
- pupils identified as walking early and not crawling;
- poor pencil control;
- difficulties in threading and any small, fine movement;
- use of scissors and following a line;
- developing a dominant hand;
- dressing skills may be slow or clothes put on in the wrong order.

Rhythm:

- poor co-ordination in dance, clapping or following and identifying beats, e.g. hitting a drum to a rhythm.

Orientation and direction:

- difficulties with left/right knowledge;
- putting cards, objects in reverse order;
- ordering right to left rather than left to right;
- no preference for using either the left or right hand.

In discussions with parents it may be discovered that:

- the child walked early and missed out on the crawling stage. Crawling is recognised as being a developmental process which aids other areas of development and its absence is considered by some to be an indicator of possible later problems;
- colour recognition and colour discrimination can also be a problem. These may be a naming or recall difficulty or a visual one. Dyslexics can be colour blind; colour blindness does not indicate dyslexia.

Pupils with the above difficulties will need more help with and additional practice in:

- ball skills;
- walking;
- balancing;
- using play equipment;
- dancing songs and actions;
- nursery rhymes;
- stories and listening games;
- memory games;
- naming and possibly word and letter order when talking;
- sequencing and copying blocks of different colours, shapes, patterns;
- threading beads;
- sorting and classifying;
- holding pencils and copying;
- organising of materials and self.

Identification in the primary school

Aspects for identification

Strengths may include:

- spatial skills;
- building and making;
- oral language;
- sport;
- non-verbal activities.

Weaknesses may include:

- memory;
- concentration work that involves recall of sequencing;
- difficulties in recalling information;
- difficulties in following instructions;
- difficulties in literacy (reading, spelling, writing);
- increasing difficulties in organisational skills.

Reading:

- difficulties in developing a sight vocabulary;
- problems in phonological development – can't match/remember the sound that goes with the letter shape;
- difficulties in blending sounds;
- little or no use of any taught strategies for decoding words;
- slow decoding, often letter by letter;
- problems in recalling the story, or part of the story;
- dislikes and/or problems in reading aloud, reading lacks fluency, accuracy;
- omissions of words;
- additions of extra letters or words, or complete 'made-up' words/sentences;
- mispronounces words;
- problems recalling letter rules which help pronunciation;
- lack of fluency affecting comprehension of reading;
- little or no expression.

Verbal responses:

- difficulties in self-expression, explanation, responses that involve an order of events.

Spelling:

- bizarre spellings – little to no relationship between the word and the letters used;
- letters in the wrong order;
- can spell orally but cannot write correctly;
- same word written inconsistently throughout work;
- reverses or inverts letters (b/d/p/q/g), (m/w), (n/u);
- wrong phonemic choice of letter (v/f for th), (ch for tu as in tube);
- problems recalling spelling rules;
- problems learning and recalling irregular, non-phonic words;
- difficulties in identifying segments or syllables within a word;
- problems in isolating individual sounds, e.g. cat (c-a-t), flag (fl-a-g);
- poor symbol–sound relationships (can't write the correct letters to match with sound);
- problems with letter names and phonemic relationships.

Writing:

- writing poorly ordered and sequenced;
- words and/or phrases missed out;
- lack of punctuation;
- slow writing speed;
- messy work with lots of 'retrys' for spellings;
- written work does not match oral language skills;
- can't copy from the board.

Handwriting:

- poor motor control;
- reversals and inversions of letters;
- poor formation of letters and joining points.

Numeracy:

- problems recalling number facts;
- problems learning tables;
- problems with sequences and patterns of number;
- mental maths:
    - problems in recall;
    - problems in recall at speed;
- written work – confuses signs $+/\times$, $\div/-$;
- recall of methodology can be difficult;
- concept difficulties, e.g. time, money, place value;
- difficulties in understanding and recalling mathematical language;
- difficulties in reading and understanding instruction/information.

Motor skills:

- difficulties in fine and/or gross motor skills;
- balance difficulties;
- problems in ball skills, hand–eye co-ordination;
- slowness in dressing/undressing in PE.

Orientation and direction:

- ongoing confusion between left and right;
- working, sequencing right to left;
- ongoing reversals, inversions and sequencing difficulties.

Work and emotional behaviour:

- lacks concentration;
- poor listening;
- avoids reading, writing;
- easily distracted;
- has many word avoidance strategies;
- won't try – lacks confidence;
- often tired after seemingly little output;
- problems in organising self and work (frequently forgets books, loses work and materials);
- has poor self-esteem;
- can be withdrawn, disruptive, becomes the class clown;
- complains of being bullied, called 'thicko' or suchlike.

Emotional/behavioural elements

The above behaviours may become more extreme as pupils progress through primary school, e.g.:

- poor confidence;
- poor self-esteem increasingly observed;
- being quiet, withdrawn and easily upset;
- regular work avoidance;
- joking, showing off, inappropriate responses;
- coping procedures – swaying, and aggressive and difficult behaviours.

Incidence of bullying, especially name calling, verbal bullying, can occur; this can be happening at playtimes and unobserved occasions. School staff need to be aware of such possibilities and have strategies in place to deal with such events. Pupils do not always mention or report such incidences.

Identification in the secondary school

Aspects for identification

Most pupils will have been identified as dyslexic or having characteristics of dyslexia by their primary school. Many of the behaviours of the primary stage are still relevant as indicators (see previous pages).

Another indicator may be a low SATs result in literacy, with higher results where the pupil has had support from readers or amanuensis in maths/science. Reading and spelling scores from tests will also be poor, and be considerably lower than the pupil's chronological age.

The SENCO and heads of department should share this information with specific members of staff together with additional relevant information.

Secondary staff need to look for and be aware of the cognitive difficulties dyslexic pupils may exhibit. They should also be aware that these ongoing difficulties can aggravate inappropriate behaviours and poor self-esteem.

Strengths may include:
- spatial skills;
- creative, imaginative and practical skills;
- oral skills;
- verbal responses to questions showing good recall;
- sport or some types of sport.

Skills and strengths may have developed through specific teaching in:
- memory strategies and short-term responses;
- some spelling and reading activities;
- handwriting focus;
- organisational skills.

Weaknesses

Memory:
- problems in recalling information and facts;
- problems in recalling instructions and verbal information;
- problems in visual recall (written information on the board);
- problems in sequencing and order of information, jokes, time, number, events, procedures, written information transposed to notes;
- problems in reading and recalling;
- problems in organisation, remembering to bring books, equipment, etc.

Phonological processing and language:
- ordering ideas and use of expressive language;

- ongoing problems in decoding in reading due to phonological problems/deficits, poor blending and poor use of reading strategies;
- poor, bizarre spellings, in phonic and non-phonic words;
- difficulties in recalling language rules: reading and spelling;
- problems in reading aloud.

Sequencing

Sequencing activities/abilities are necessary in the majority of activities from writing, to movement, to dance, to timing, to ordering events, to cooking, to dressing and to cleaning teeth. Within schools, teachers need to be aware of what their subject and activity demands are in these areas, particularly in such areas as:

- writing in an ordered and structured way;
- handwriting;
- copying from the board;
- PE in co-ordinated activities (e.g. gymnastics, ball skills);
- historical events, which may not be recalled or sequenced;
- science: recall of procedure, terminology, formula;
- operational and methodological processes (cross-curricular).

Synthesising information:

- problems showing that some strategies cannot be developed as previous information is lost;
- problems in bringing information together and transferring skills and knowledge between and from previous subjects and associated subjects, e.g.:
  - maths and science (operations and formulas);
  - history and geography (time and place);
  - literacy (writing, cross-curricular);
- work (output) and responses showing that auditory and/or visual information is not being processed and interpreted, or recalled correctly;
- handwriting and copying, difficulties in transferring and collating written information;
- poor writing skills – organisation of ideas, structuring work.

Emotional/behavioural elements

Oppositional behaviour, and withdrawn or work avoidance behaviours can become more extreme in the secondary school setting. Confidence and self-esteem can also be affected. Observed behaviours may show:

- withdrawn behaviours;
- non-involvement in class;
- failure to return homework;
- poor self-esteem;
- aggression and non-compliance;
- bravado and exhibitionist behaviour rather than showing/revealing what he/she can or can't do;
- work avoidance;
- distress caused by name calling or bullying by others.

Visual dyslexia

The term 'visual dyslexia' can be found in articles and other literature. Research in this area is ongoing and the effectiveness of some of the forms of treatment is under debate. While the focus of dyslexia is on auditory and phonological coding problems, **the difficulties some dyslexic pupils have with visual processing must also be recognised**.

It is important that the term 'visual processing' is understood. Visual processing is the way the eye receives and the brain interprets information. It can also be influenced by external environmental elements. Visual processing difficulties can be seen across a range of reading and writing difficulties, some medical conditions and a range of spectrum disorders. **The term visual dyslexia should therefore not be used in a general or haphazard way**.

It should be diagnosed by a specialist in the area who can rule out disease (pathological conditions) and refractive errors (the need for glasses). An eye examination should be the first step. It is recommended that the minimum check should be:

- an assessment of the need for glasses;
- an assessment of the eye's health;
- a check on the visual standard;
- a full check on the muscle response.

(Jordan 2000)

When looking at visual processing it is important to understand the role of the eye within reading.

The four elements of the eye are:

- good eyesight;
- eyes that work together;
- good focus;
- good directional movement.

Breakdowns within some or all of these areas will cause problems in reading and writing – particularly copying. The eyes may not move together, or fixate on something close. They may move or jump around the text (saccadic eye movement) and focus (accommodation) can be difficult. There can be difficulties following a moving object, e.g. a ball. There may also be acuity and perception problems.

External factors can be alleviated as can effects from external elements, such as lighting, which can cause flicker problems below 350 Hz and pattern glare. Computers and televisions can also cause flicker problems in the peripheral vision. For colour blindness there are special contact lenses (ChromaGen Lenses) which have a different colour spot in each lens.

Identifiable symptoms of poor visual processing include:

- reading/writing difficulties;
- reversals of words, letters and/or numbers (was/saw), (on/no), (d/p/q), (3/2/5), (9/6/8);
- sequential difficulties with letters (these are often visual rather than memory deficits);
- fixation problems;
- blurring of print;
- movement or vibration of words or letters;
- problems with copying (again these are often visual rather than memory deficits);
- visual memory problems;
- tracking difficulties;
- hearing or balancing problems;
- holding a book at an unusual angle;
- closing one eye while reading;
- watery eyes;
- migraine or frontal headaches;
- eye rubbing during reading;
- reduced visual acuity;
- reduced accommodation or convergence;
- difficulties catching a ball;
- problems with light and pattern glare;
- difficulties with concentration.

Any child who appears not to concentrate should be assessed, as should all children who are significantly behind relative to their ability.

Appendix 5 (extract from *Visual Dyslexia: A Guide for Parents and Teachers*, Jordan 2000) identifies ages when symptoms may be observed. These ages are indicators and not rigid.

Eye specialists may be optomologists or orthoptists, although there are overlaps between the specialists in some areas.

An optomologist's (ophthalmic optician's) work will focus on coloured lenses, filters and overlays. He/she will also investigate accommodation lag and fixation disparity lag.

An orthoptist will look at co-ordination between acuity, binocular vision and fusion reserves, and accommodation. Some will also look at the need for colour overlays and use an Intuitive Colorimeter.

Treatments can be divided into areas that look at the use of:

- coloured spectacles;
- coloured overlays;

- contact lenses (with/without colour spots) (Irten Syndrome, Crium Overlays, Intuitive Colorimeter, ChromaGen Lenses);
- eye exercises;
- magnifiers (glasses, magnifying glass, visual tracking magnifiers, visual line readers);
- occlusion (patching, semi/stenopaic slits);
- prisms.

Suggestions to parents and schools may include:
- diet modification;
- fatty acid supplements;
- memory building exercises;
- auditory strategies;
- lighting modifications to reduce pattern glare;
- computer screen filter;
- change of seating location;
- modification to worksheet (print size, spacing, font, paper colour);
- no copying from the board;
- reduced copying generally;
- support with visual tracking – eye movement following a pen/finger; covering of text above/below that being read.

These suggestions are not exhaustive; additional information can be found in a range of literature and websites. The British Association of Behavioural Optometrists and The Institute of Optometry also provide information (see Useful addresses).

In recognising symptoms of visual processing difficulties, discussions with the pupil, parents and other professionals involved with the pupil are important.

For the pupil, questions relating to print such as 'do words move?' can give insight into how he/she sees print. The pupil who has always seen print move, wobble or blur may think that this is normal.

External agencies may be able to offer advice and suggestions but it should be eye specialists who make the diagnosis and offer specialist recommendations. Referrals can be made via GPs to specialist centres; alternatively, specialists in optometrics will advise and give local names and numbers of optomologists/orthoptists who have an interest/knowledge of dyslexia.

There are a growing number of trials, of various forms of treatment, which focus on specific areas of visual processing difficulties. These may come to the fore in the near future.

Emotional issues

Confronted with failure and criticism, the usual responses of individuals are flight or fight.

Consequently for the dyslexic pupil, responses may be either:

- **flight** – where involvement in class activities, and general or independent learning is avoided; or
- **fight** – where frustration gives rise to inappropriate forms of behaviour.

Other issues that may arise are instances of:

- **bullying** (verbal or physical);
- **resentment**;
- **sustaining positive peer relationships**.

Low self-esteem and low motivation are more evident as the child grows older and there are greater expectations on performance.

Suggestions for general approaches to raise self-esteem and motivation

- Show understanding of pupils' problems.
- Discuss problems and find solutions.
- For older pupils, discuss dyslexia and what it means.
- Identify strengths; point out that some famous people are dyslexic.
- Give reassurance.
- Discuss dyslexia with parents.
- Talk to other professionals if necessary.
- Show that you recognise any bullying and deal with it.
- Use class opportunities: circle time, and Personal, Social and Health Education (PSHE) to raise peer understanding.
- Look at your own teaching and modify and extend your style.
- Provide positive learning opportunities.
- Listen to the pupil.

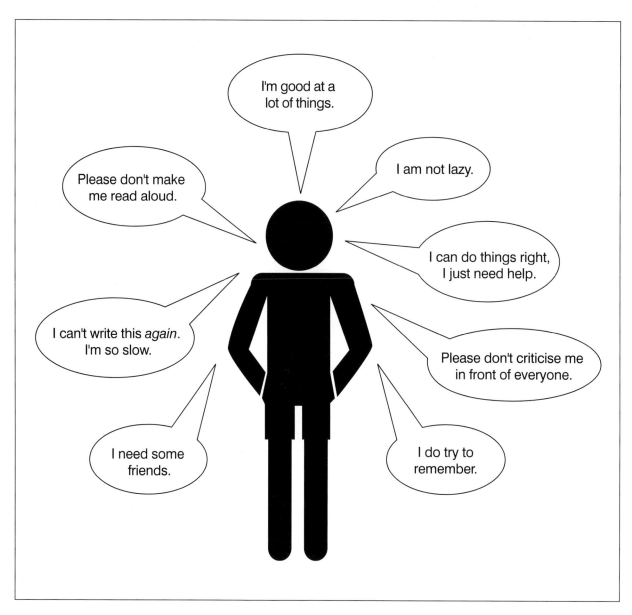

Talk to and try to understand dyslexic pupils

Approaches to aid learning

People have different strengths and preferences when learning. Learning comes via the senses.

Pupils with dyslexia learn best when all the senses are used. Learning and teaching become:

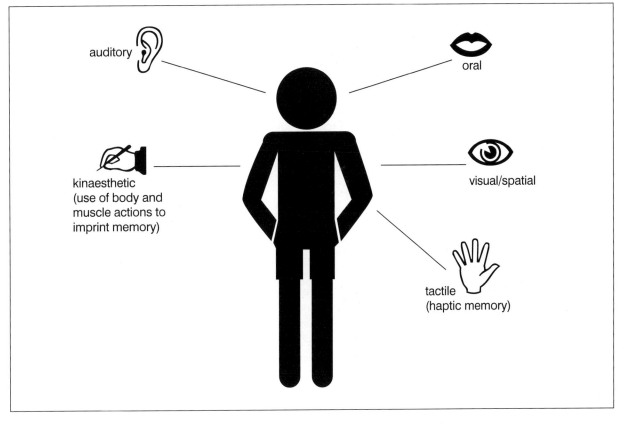

auditory

oral

kinaesthetic
(use of body and
muscle actions to
imprint memory)

visual/spatial

tactile
(haptic memory)

Multi-sensory

This may be referred to as Visual, Auditory, Kinaesthetic learning (VAK).

It is important to teach to dyslexic pupils' strengths and support weaker areas. Observations and assessments can identify both.

The government outlined skills to develop learning in the National Curriculum 2000 (Key Stages 1 and 2 – see Appendix 6). These have been categorised as 'thinking skills', knowing and learning how to learn; and 'key skills', skills identified as improving learning and performance for work and life. Within the thinking skills are:

- Information processing
- Reasoning
- Enquiry
- Creativity
- Evaluation

The area that dyslexic pupils may need most support with is that of information processing. Other areas may need prompting and structuring; at the same time they can enhance and focus dyslexic pupils' oral, deductive and creative skills, in which they can succeed.

Within the key skills are:

- Communication
- Application of number
- Information technology
- Working with others
- Problem solving
- Improving their own learning/performance.

These skills come into play in all areas of the curriculum particularly in Key Stages 3 and 4 when the development of effective study skills is so important. Pupils with dyslexia will need appropriate encouragement and support if they are to fulfil their potential.

Research and models of learning are ongoing. Within the identification of Multiple Intelligences, Howard Gardner looks at eight learning styles; other authorities identify a greater number of intelligences (skills and strengths).

Gardner identifies people's strengths in regard to learning as:

- **Interpersonal**
- **Intrapersonal**
- **Mathematical and logical**
- **Visual and spatial**
- **Kinaesthetic**
- **Musical**
- **Naturalistic**
- **Linguistic**

Many people have elements of some or all of the above.

For the dyslexic pupil, there will be a greater imbalance of strengths and skills. An awareness of all learning styles may help teachers develop areas of pupils' strengths by varying teaching approaches and methods.

Learning itself will benefit from the simultaneous interaction of all sensory areas: oral, visual, auditory, tactile and kinaesthetic – a multi-sensory approach.

Learning pathways

Other authorities focus on strengthening learning by trying to 'connect' learning pathways, leading to the development of educational kinesiology. This looks at the science of body movement in relation to brain function, leading to the development of a series of movements called 'Brain Gym', which concentrates on laterality, centring and focus. These exercises can be taught to individuals or to groups; some schools have adopted such approaches following specialist training.

More recently there have been developments and research based on findings from NASA and research into the cerebellum. Again, focus is on the areas of balance and co-ordination and the way the cerebrum processes movement information. The Dyslexia, Dyspraxia and Attention Disorders Treatment Centre (DDAT) (see Useful addresses) uses technology from which a series of individual specific exercises are produced following a series of assessments.

These more specialist approaches, where emphasis is placed on the study of Cerebellar Developmental Delay and remediation via exercises, are proving effective for both adults and children.

Information on Neuro-Development Therapy can be obtained from the Developmental Practitioners' Association (see Useful addresses).

For some dyslexic pupils these alternative strategies are beneficial. They will work alongside strategies that strengthen phonological coding, reading and writing. It is important to think of dyslexia as being more than just a language disability.

Other learning skills will be necessary for working in other areas of the curriculum and in accessing skills for living.

The dyslexic pupil needs opportunities to:
- develop his/her preferred learning style;
- work to his/her strengths;
- be supported in areas of weakness;
- have specific teaching;
- be given demonstrated strategies to aid learning.

Specific strategies for teaching

Direct teaching will be necessary for some of the strategies identified below. These strategies will also benefit other pupils. Pupils need to be shown 'how' to learn spellings, e.g. Read, Remember, Write (RRW); Simultaneous Oral Spelling (SOS); Look, Say, Cover, Write, Check (LSCWC); all of which involve memory.

Many of the strategies may be cross-curricular and used at times for homework and revision. They include memory, phonological development, auditory and visual discrimination, and sequencing. They can be built up over time and across Key Stages; some are more relevant to Key Stages 1 and 2, others for Key Stage 3.

Memory

- Activities that develop visual and auditory memory

  These may be objects, colours, shapes, letters, anything that involves recall. Initially work with a small number, gradually increasing number or instructions. Some can be played as games:
  - Kim's Game
  - What's Missing? (remove items)
  - What's Changed? (re-sequence items)
  - Listen Games (e.g. I went to the… and got…)
  - Listen and Repeat (nursery rhymes)
  - Follow Verbal Instructions (1-, 2-, 3-part)
  - Songs (alphabet, rainbow, etc.)

- Read, Remember, Write (RRW)

  This can apply to words but usually consists of short sentences. It links with memory work and should contain words the pupil has previously learned. It is also a strategy that is useful when copying from a worksheet (copying from a blackboard should be avoided). The pupil reads the word or phrase, covers and writes. This can also be done with a Language Master and some computer programs.

- Dictation-type exercises using *known* words also aid auditory memory skills. It is important not to dictate too quickly. The pupil has to listen, take the information in, find the correct letter order/word response and then write it down while listening to the next piece of information. Adjust your approach to the needs of the pupil.

Phonological development

- Multi-sensory teaching of individual letters/sound groups on a one-to-one basis, following a structure recommended by the Dyslexia Institute or specifically designed dyslexia materials/resources, are established approaches. These will focus on the development of reading and/or spelling cards which build cumulatively on the teaching of sounds.

Cards show lower- and upper-case letters on one side:

and on the other side a word and sound (in brackets) with associated picture, drawn by the pupil:

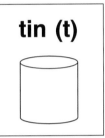

The pupil has to learn and repeat the association word and correct sound, and the letter/s to be written when the word is given, e.g.:

 Pupil says 'black (bl)' when reading; when pupil writing, adult says 'black (bl)' and the pupil says 'bl' or 'b.l.' and writes b.l.

Pupils should be encouraged to say the letter names when writing/spelling as letters, not sounds, are written.

Vowels

It is important that the vowels are taught. This may be on a different-coloured card, via mnemonics or any way that prompts learning and recall.

Auditory and visual discrimination

Auditory discrimination focuses on listening and identifying phonemes, the position of phonemes, or patterns and groups of phonemes in a word. Alternative sounds can be used, e.g. duck quacking, cat meowing, to develop listening skills.

- Develop activities that involve perception and discrimination such as, Where do you hear the sound...? (beginning, middle or end of a word), syllable work, beats in a word, word segmentation (as syllables or compound words), odd-man-out in a group of rhyming words.

Visual discrimination focuses on visual patterns, orientation and sequence.

- Tracking involves finding a given letter, word or sentence from a range of letters, words or sentences in each line. Tracking a sequence of symbolic or non-symbolic cards, with a focus on orientation, can also be used.

Both auditory and visual areas should be developed and/or strengthened.

Tracking

Tracking letters

For example, tracking the letter c – the pupil says 'c' (c) as he/she circles the letter:

a f ⓒ z y ⓒ o m n ⓒ

ⓒ p u w ⓒ p l ⓒ a b

Tracking words

For example, tracking the word 'went' – the pupil says 'went – w-e-n-t' (letter names) as he/she circles the word:

and (went) out (went) by

(went) for when (went) so

be (went) wheel was (went)

Sequencing

Our lives are governed by sequences: movement, time (calendar time and analogue and digital time) events, dressing, stories, jokes, numbers, letters, words, etc. are all sequenced and ordered.

To help develop sequencing skills some activities can be practised and some taught:

- Sequenced physical movements can be built up in small steps and in early games and action songs, e.g. Simon Says; Head, Shoulders, Knees and Toes.
- Teach days of the week, months of the year, the alphabet.
- Sequencing within learning, e.g. the alphabet, sentences, events, numbers and physical routines, will be ongoing.

With co-ordinated, sequenced activities such as action songs, games, dances, e.g. hokey-cokey, or aerobics the pupil/student will have to keep a sequence, rhythm and knowledge of left/right balanced.

To help dyslexic pupils/students:

- Teach sequencing in stages.
- Have someone directly in front or to the side for the pupil to follow/copy.
- Provide a strategy to remember left/right.

In other areas 'chunk' pieces of information and learn as small groups and sections.

Oral rehearsal, talking through the activity and/or information as it is being done, will help internalise and aid recall.

Using the alphabet as a learning tool

Ideas for using letters to learn the alphabet and other activities are indicated here. The 'rainbow' shape is used as it allows the pupil to sit directly in front of the letter M and N, which are at the centre of the alphabet. The pupil can also access the letters easily.

The usefulness of wooden/plastic letters cannot be overestimated. They are versatile and can be found in upper- and lower-case. Upper-case letters eliminate confusion. Two sets of each are useful, for words with double letters, etc. Upper- and lower-case sets can also be matched.

Visual placement of letters in an arc

- Work should be 'paired' with the teacher and pupil working together. Gradually the pupil should become more confident and be able to place the letters independently.
- It can be learned in chunks (abcd-efg-hijk-lmno-pqr-stu-vw-xyz), sung as the letters are placed, touched and said/sung on completion of part of or the whole alphabet.

  (If the alphabet is to be taught in chunks, one method is to use only the letters currently being worked on and known letters.)

- When initially sorting the letters prior to placing, check all letters are the right way round. Sometimes, to help organisation, split the letters into:

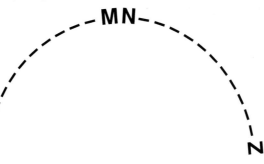

a at the front;
z at the end;
mn in the middle.

Other letters can be sorted into left or right group of MN.

- Some pupils may benefit initially from an alphabet strip to copy from, if they find this exercise difficult.

Alphabet and vowel placement to practise sound and word building

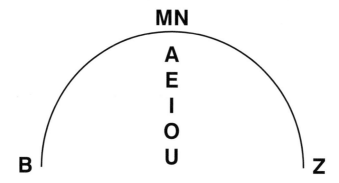

- The pupil will need to be able to learn and distinguish both long and short vowel sounds and learn patterns of words using vowels (v) and consonants (c).

Letter patterns include:

- cv – consonant, vowel;
- vc – vowel, consonant;
- cvcc – consonant, vowel, consonant, consonant;
- ccvc – consonant, consonant, vowel, consonant;
- cvccvc – consonant, vowel, consonant, consonant, vowel, consonant.

Other uses of the alphabet can include:

- dictionary and general alphabetical work;
- auditory and visual memory games (The pupil either sees or hears a given number of letters (from 2 to 8). The pupil repeats and then physically sequences and orientates the letters.);
- phonic work;
- vowel and blending work;
- word building;
- segmenting words and sounds.

Spelling

- Spellings can range from giving one letter (linked to sounds and names), phonic/non-phonic words, to subject-specific words.
- Some authorities believe that starting pupils from an early age with cursive handwriting aids spelling. This is because certain letter groups always go together and conversely others do not. The flow of the hand helps to overcome sequencing and orientation problems. Schools will need to discuss 'handwriting' within a whole-school approach.
- When learning spellings the maximum number of words given to secure success should be 7. This is based on spelling and memory research. For some pupils this may be too many; they need to start with 1–3 words of 1, 2 or 3 letters.

When giving spellings to learn:

- Do not give pupils long words of 6–7 letters in length if their working memory will only recall 4 letters.
- Give phonic and non-phonic words separately where possible.
- Look at spelling patterns.
- Identify the syllables.
- Teach any spelling rules.
- Demonstrate Look, Say, Cover, Write, Check (LSCWC) methods.
- Demonstrate Simultaneous Oral Spelling (SOS).

To teach SOS the teacher should:

- present the words on a card;
- say the word.

The pupil should then:

- say the word;
- say each letter name as he/she writes the word;
- check to see if the word has been written correctly;
- repeat the procedure periodically and regularly until the spelling is known confidently.

Understanding text

The complexity of printed information and the depth of understanding required will increase as the pupil progresses through the levels of the National Curriculum.

Various techniques can be used to improve understanding of printed text. To develop these the pupil needs to be taught the skills of:

- Note taking (highlighting, abbreviating and underlining)
- Drawing and interpreting:
    - Flow charts
    - Spidergrams and mind maps
    - Note lines
    - Tables
    - Charts
    - Graphs

Helpful techniques include **SQ3R** (Survey, Question, Read, Recall, Review). This helps the pupil to understand new information. It involves a structured sequence of activities:

Survey

Question

Read

Recall

Review

Survey:

- The pupil reads through the information quite quickly; he/she may experience significant difficulties with this.
- Key words which identify the main point of the text are identified.
- The words are written down, underlined or highlighted.

Question:

The pupil formulates and records questions about the information:

- Who/what is the information about?
- What happened?
- Where did it happen?
- When did it happen?
- How did it happen?
- Why did it happen?

The pupil is given time to consider possible answers.

Read:

- The pupil reads through the information slowly and carefully.
- Important points are identified and emphasised.

Recall:

- The pupil tries to remember and explain the information.
- The pupil tries to draw any diagrams, tables or charts from memory.

Review:

- The pupil reads the text again. The accuracy and completeness of answers are checked.
- The pupil makes any further notes.

DARTS

Directed
Activities
Related to
Text

This offers the pupil alternative ways to identify important points in the text. It focuses on fostering reading as a thinking tool.

The teacher provides:

- a blank chart or table for recording information;
- a set of prompt questions to help the selection of information;
- a cloze procedure exercise to record the information.

The pupil:

- picks out the main points by highlighting or underlining;
- writes brief notes on the highlighted key points;
- sorts information into sets of similar points;
- uses headings and subheadings to label paragraphs;
- rewrites information in the newly summarised form;
- presents the information in a different form: a chart or diagram instead of continuous prose.

Advanced reading strategies

This is a course which that to improve reading techniques rather than overcome fundamental difficulties.

It is a focused 12-hour programme for Key Stage 4 students, run as 4 x 3-hour sessions. It is activity based and individually paced.

The programme concentrates on:

- developing flexible reading strategies;
- improving comprehension;
- increasing the speed of reading to over 165 words a minute – below which comprehension is difficult to achieve.

Outcomes include:

- improved reading speed and comprehension;
- improved examination performances;
- improved motivation, confidence and self-esteem;
- reversals in the demotivating effects of earlier failure;
- reduced stress and fatigue.

Such approaches may benefit the dyslexic student who has achieved a level of reading from previously practised strategies. This develops and supports approaches such as SQ3R and DARTS, and the higher order skills of skimming and scanning.

Skills developed include:

- previewing;
- chunking;
- paragraphing;
- efficient use of peripheral vision;
- reading for meaning;
- decision-making.

Other similar strategies can be tried such as Preview, Question, Read, Summarise (PQRS). This also focuses on reading, ranging from picture cues and headings, to skimming and scanning, word segmentation, and syntactic and semantic analysis.

Helping pupils to help themselves

Within the approaches to aid learning dyslexic pupils can be taught how to record and recall information that can help them become more successful and independent within the learning process. They can be taught to develop:

Interest   by looking for something interesting in everything that has to be learned.

Understanding   by questioning what is not understood.

Confidence   by thinking positively.

Concentration   by making simple notes or pictures.

Overlearning   by revision and repeated practice.

Rehearsal   by repeating aloud what has to be remembered.

Mnemonics   by using the initial letters of words to recall a sequence.

Chunking   by putting information into bits or chunks; these may include numbers (phone), letters (alphabet/words).

Chanting   by using rhyme and rhythm in arranging information.

Mind maps   by using words or other symbols to represent information. The layout reinforces the connections between the key points. It supports selection, recording, sorting and recall.

Metacognition strategies   by consciously asking questions such as:
- How will I remember this?
- What was easy/difficult?
- How did I/will I do this?
- Have I done it before and how did I do it?
- Is there a quicker/easier way? etc.

Oral rehearsal strategies   This links with metacognition. It involves talking through what is to be learned and will cover most activities, e.g.:
- Writing a word – by saying it before or as writing; the mouth forms letters which the ear hears and the brain interprets more easily.
- Repeating a sequence of movements, operations, facts and rules, etc.
- Repeating or talking through sequences or operations as the body is carrying out the activity.

Automaticity   The ability to respond automatically. Give overlearning and practice to the particular skill so that it is internalised.

Some curriculum implications

Implications for certain curriculum areas can be identified.

Reading and writing problems will encompass most curriculum areas. Other elements of curricular expectations and knowledge/skill areas need to be considered. These will include:	
PE	• changing time, dressing skills, organisation/storage of clothes to prevent loss • sequential co-ordinated movements • ball skills (throwing/catching) • some gross motor skills
Music	• rhythm and beats • recall of sequences • auditory perception areas
Geography	• linking definitions with the correct geographical terminology • written work – independent or copied
RE	• recall of certain facts within a time frame • sequence of events • written work – independent or copied
History	• recall of dates and major events • sequential elements within a time frame • understanding of time • written work – independent or copied
Science	• recall of formula – orientation of numbers • application of the right approach • sequence of the experimental process • following instructions • recall of the correct definition for subject-specific vocabulary • recording
Maths	• use of correct method • orientation of numbers • recognising similar operational symbols • recall of tables • learning sequential information • recording calculations

The areas identified here are not exhaustive; knowledge of the individual will identify other areas of difficulty.

Differentiation

The National Curriculum states that it may be necessary to choose *"knowledge, skills and understanding from earlier or later key stages… there may not be time to teach all aspects of age-related programmes of study."* It is important, however, to have high but realistic expectations of pupils.

In any input/teaching, analysing the approach of teaching, task and learning should help differentiation.

Differentiation should support all pupils. Some forms of differentiation are more essential for dyslexic pupils.

Some aspects of differentiation which include essentials for dyslexic pupils are identified below. An analysis of teacher input and task analysis, together with pupils' difficulties and possible strategies, is important in supporting dyslexia. It is useful to divide differentiation into broad and practical strategies, as:

1. General aspects of differentiation.
2. Analysis of dyslexic pupils' difficulties and needs against the tasks.

1. Differentiation: general aspects

Learning and teaching styles:

- Be aware of an individual's learning style and teach accordingly, e.g. logical, visual, practical (doer); musical, linguistic, naturalist, etc.
- Combine all learning styles to produce a multi-sensory style of approaches to both teaching and learning.
- Develop thinking skills to aid learning and responses.
- Refer to Appendix 6 key skills sheet.

Management of presentation:

- Avoid copying from a board – provide pre-written notes (again check presentation and amounts of information).
- Supply lists of key words – subject-specific words (and give to support staff, who can also give a brief overview of the lesson and expectations if appropriate).
- Give pupils questions at the appropriate level (i.e. which are not too complex in length or content).
- Materials should be at the appropriate readability level and language level.
- Use less information on a page, with appropriate size of print or font.
- Present information in different ways (include diagrams, key headings, visual cues, arrow/flow charts).

Resources:

- Identify pupils who need a specific amount of additional adult support; identify the type of support – adult, materials, ICT.
- Use technology resources – Language Masters, computers, tape recorders, dictaphones; give pupils time to learn how to use.
- Differentiate resources, worksheets.
- Have resources that link subject-specific vocabulary with concepts and definitions.

Time:

- Give pupils time to reflect.
- Offer additional time for tasks.
- Allow time to absorb information, gather materials and complete work.
- Give thinking time when questioning.

Assessment:

- Recognise the degree of effort demanded, to enable a pupil to carry out a task.
- Examine what it is you are assessing, e.g. knowledge of concept, and grade accordingly.
- Grade for effort if possible.

Management of the task:

- Consider groupings: collaborative working in pairs or groups which will allow different pupils to work to their strengths.
- Break tasks down into appropriate steps.
- Give alternative ways of recording (diagrams, mind maps, flow charts, tape recorders, ICT links, discussion, etc.).

Management of room:

- Check that the layout of the room is 'dyslexia-friendly' – students sitting in the best place for access, seeing and using resources.
- Decide on seating arrangement that benefits the student.

2. Differentiation: practical strategies for the teacher

(a) Analysis of teacher input
(b) Task analysis

Differentiation looks at the considerations the teacher must make to the lesson input (a) and the expectations made of pupils (b). The strategies are those to be employed to help the pupils.

(a) Analysis of teacher input

Teacher input	Pupil's difficulty	Strategy
Giving verbal information	• auditory memory • rate of processing information • recall of facts	• reduce talking time • give small amounts of information • focus on key information • restructure personal language; sentence length and complexity • give time for assimilation of information • ask questions • give visual information • give learning/memory tips
Presenting visual information – words, sentences, pictures, map	• visual memory • readability level 16* • eye movements • rate of processing information • comprehension	• talk/read through information • present material and check understanding • ask questions • highlight key points • give pupils own copy if the work is on the board • give learning time • give learning tips • give memory tips
Asking questions	• recall of facts • processing of the questions	• give prompts of prior knowledge • prompt metacognitive strategies • give clear, precise questions • give clues to aid recall • give answering time

*The readability level is the reading level/age of the text as against the pupil's reading age.

(b) Task analysis

Consider the lesson content, task/activity and expectations.

Task	Pupil's difficulty	Teaching strategy
Responding to questions	• analysis of questions • recall of facts • organisation of internal information and verbalising	• prompt as to when/how work was done • ask questions to aid memory • repeat questions • ensure questions are clear and precise
Reading	• decoding skills • phonological knowledge • visual memory • eye movements	• teach a variety of decoding skills • use multi-sensory approaches • structure methods to phonological approaches (reading and spelling, e.g. British Dyslexia Association (BDA) structure) • use regular overlearning • use age-appropriate text • reduce area of focus • use coloured overlays

Task	Pupil's difficulty	Teaching strategy
Writing		
• organisation of ideas	• memory	• pupil to verbalise before he/she starts
	• sequencing	• use mind mapping
		• identify key points
• spelling, punctuation	• sound–symbol correspondence	• identify starting points
		• use subject vocabulary lists

	• sequencing memory	• use:
		  – dictionaries
		  – spellchecks
		  – word processors

		• teach strategies/rules
		• reinforce/reinforcement time
• legibility	• fine motor skills	• practise computer/ keyboard skills
• dictation	• automaticity in skills	• give limited amounts of dictation
• lot of copying from board (or notes)	• eye movements, place/orientation, motor skills	• provide short, concise notes
		• provide notes with main points highlighted
		• put number sentences on the board – pupil puts corresponding numbers in a book as he/she copies
Handwriting	• motor control	• teach cursive script with structured, sequential teaching
		• use cursive-style wooden letters in a multi-sensory way to trace and tell the hand where to move – link with name and sound
		• link with reading-spelling programme

Task	Pupil's difficulty	Teaching strategy
Sorting information	• reading age • identification of key points/ability to process useful information • ability to process useful information	• reduce readability levels and amounts of information • highlight specific information • sort ICT facilities
Holding information	• memory • sequencing	• encourage metacognitive strategies • use learning strengths • identify key points • present multi-sensory approaches • give time to process information • allow different ways of encoding, e.g. diagrammatically, orally
Reading information	• phonological processing • visual memory • sequencing	• check readability levels • use paired reading • tape information • reduce amount of information • highlight key points

Task	Pupil's difficulty	Teaching strategy
Maths		
• language of maths	• short-term working memory	• use overlearning
• learning tables	• reading/language	• discuss written maths problem
• recognising symbols	• sequencing (learning direction, orientation)	
• writing numbers and setting out	• spatial organisation	• use vocabulary work
• reading	• visual discrimination	
• mental maths	• recall	• write out process – some pupils benefit from linking the vocabulary and symbol together; cards can be given to learn
		• explain working process
		• use different colours for place value
• problem-solving	• recall of methodologies	• use practical aids/work
		• use method cards
		• use spreadsheets
		• use 100-square grid
		• use ICT
		• use multi-sensory approaches
		• chunk information when learning, e.g. tables
		• use prompt cards for methods
		• offer additional time for processing
		• link process (symbol) with definition. Give cards to learn, and put up in classrooms as prompts

$$+$$

add
more than
addition
increase
....
....

ICT to support curriculum access

Both dyslexic and other pupils can use technology and ICT skills to develop and aid learning. **Dyslexic pupils can benefit from any technology that reinforces multi-sensory learning.**

These include:

- Language Masters
- Computers and specific software
- Dictaphones
- Tape recorders

Computers can offer a range of support structures; these may include:

- arranging information in sequential order (spreadsheets);
- presenting information in graphic form;
- filing subject-specific vocabulary and definitions, colour coded for phonic recognition along with digital sound (pupils can transfer information to a piece of work via multi-sensory methods – read, listen, do, re-check);
- word processing facilities (particularly text to speech);
- presentation of work – choice of colour, style and font size;
- voice recognition to allow for dictation;
- overlearning – drill and practice software;
- memory games;
- programs to develop lateral thinking/problem-solving;
- accessing text via scanning – text to speech.

While ICT will be taught sequentially through the primary system, dyslexic pupils will still need to work on specific skills over and above other pupils. These may include:

- very early development of keyboard skills;
- practice of keyboard skills;
- practice of system routines;
- strategies to develop ideas and vocabulary to be used and transferred to writing and word processing work;
- sequential thinking and clarity of ideas;
- focus on key information;
- use of speech to text facilities (oral skills).

Teacher support

If word processing facilities are used to develop worksheets, care needs to be taken to:

- keep information short and specific;
- colour or change fonts to identify key elements;
- vary font size (double spacing may be useful);
- include context-led illustration if appropriate.

Programs such as Encarta may need transcribed pages if a hard copy is wanted, as the presentation and readability levels may not be appropriate. Alternatively, access to text can be used via a text to speech program.

The internet is a useful tool. See Appendix 8 for addresses, information and software.

Supporting pupils at Key Stages 3–4

New pupils can become lost, late for lessons and have forgotten homework, books, etc. Dyslexic pupils may find greater difficulty than most due to poor memory, orientation and organisational skills.

To access new environments, routines and expectations, additional specific information needs to be given and home–school liaison opportunities developed, to allow the home to set up support strategies.

Initial school strategies should include:

- a map of the school with colour coded information as to room locations/subject faculties;
- names of staff linked to the colour coded information;
- timetables, again with colour coded links;
- daily diaries and/or homework diaries with specific messages and information, some of which may link with room location, and days where specific equipment should be in school, e.g. books, PE kit;
- a buddy system can also be useful.

Colour coding is useful, as it allows visual scanning and reading and develops links to aid memory.

Note: Some dyslexic pupils are also colour blind and reds/greens can be a problem.

Good practice includes:

- all subject staff knowing who the dyslexic pupils are;
- having an understanding of dyslexia, with possible strengths, weaknesses and implications for their subject;
- knowledge of individual pupils' strengths and weaknesses;
- introduction of lesson objectives;
- differentiation;
- presentation of information in an accessible way;
- cues for recall;
- multi-sensory approaches;
- reductions in and alternatives to copying.

Overall:

- instructions should be clearly written;
- expectations and information should be made explicit;
- pupils should be helped to formulate and respond to questions;
- oral assessment opportunities should be given.

As pupils move through secondary school more focus will be needed to support them in:

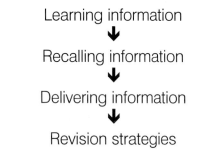

Learning information

⬇

Recalling information

⬇

Delivering information

⬇

Revision strategies

This will include teachers/other adults and pupils developing:

- An understanding of learning styles
- Memory strategies
- Metacognitive strategies
- Multi-sensory approaches

Learning information via:

- presenting material in a variety of ways;
- reducing teacher talk time – keep to objectives;
- giving examples of general and specific concepts;
- using spreadsheets;
- mind mapping approaches;
- chunking information;
- linking subject-specific words with definitions;
- diagrammatic and/or flow chart work;
- using mnemonics;
- giving oral rehearsal of task (talk through);
- giving ICT opportunities;
- practising to consolidate new skills;
- overlearning information;
- discussing with pupil to help internalisation of information;
- questioning pupil to gauge understanding.

Recalling information via:

- giving additional thinking/processing and writing time;
- giving aids and prompts (visual/auditory);
- encouraging recall of mind maps/flow charts;
- using metacognitive strategies;
- providing linkage/association opportunities;
- linking cross-curricular knowledge, prior knowledge;
- giving practice opportunities for exam revising responses;
- encouraging oral rehearsal in learning;
- demonstrating a variety of memory techniques.

Delivering information via:

- modelling or prompting pupils when eliciting oral responses to get clear and specific answers;
- giving strategies to aid confidence in oral/written responses;
- demonstrating approaches and giving examples of different approaches (oral and written);
- giving exam practice and showing examples of approaches.

Work placements

The skills that dyslexic students may have should be utilised via work placements. Such skills could include:

- visual–spatial development;
- design;
- practical aspects;
- looking at the whole picture, e.g. necessary end result;
- lateral, non-conformist approaches to problems – good problem-solving.

Tutors need to make the placement providers aware of:

- dyslexic pupils and those who may have similar characteristics;
- skills and strengths of dyslexic students;
- needs and areas of support.

Placements should where possible link with students' strengths, enabling the building of confidence and the development of self-esteem.

Placement providers may, however, need to be given specific information to enable them, with the tutor's support, to overcome such difficulties as:

- following written instructions and manuals;
- following oral instructions/information that is long or complex;
- sequencing information, recalling messages and telephone numbers;
- writing and message taking;
- filing and organisation of information;
- organisation of self and others;
- telling the time and time keeping (organisation of self);
- left/right problems;
- mathematical language (written and symbolic).

Placements where possible should:

- be of a practical nature to support students' strengths and interests;
- have regular routines, tasks and structures;
- give information in chunks/small steps and in a variety of ways;
- ensure information and expectations are expressed overtly, not implied;
- have expectations and routines regularly revisited and checked for understanding;
- have additional time given in order to complete or consolidate new tasks;
- set up 'paired' situations within the placement, with an experienced co-worker;
- allow opportunities to think laterally;

- provide opportunities to develop problem-solving;
- have the necessary resources to support students' work.

Teachers need to discuss with students the benefits of telling future employers that they are dyslexic.

There are a number of significant considerations to be made with regard to both employment and the Disability Discrimination Act (1995). The SEN and Disability Act (2001) (SENDA) can also be used as a reference, as can the Human Rights Act (2000). More advice may need to be sought in this area.

Summary of skills development

Subject	Skill areas to develop
Literacy/reading	• phonic development (linked with spelling) • overlearning sight vocabulary (subject-specific and keywords) • decoding strategies • speed reading • skimming/scanning for specific information
Writing (spelling)	• development of phoneme (sound) and grapheme (written letter) correspondence • increased use of letter names • confident use of word segmentation • learning spelling rules and practice with specific examples • focus on subject-specific and keywords • use of a variety of spelling strategies
Handwriting	• overall practice of letter formation • automaticity of letter shape with name and sound • cursive style of writing • identification of mistakes, showing correct responses
Speed writing/typing (to aid responses in exams)	• if copying, recall of groups of letters in chunks, transcribing as many as possible without looking • practice in dictation, helpful if kept to known and familiar words • increased automaticity in spelling, confidence speeds up the flow of writing • clear thinking, knowing what is wanted prior to the beginning of writing – using notes, diagrams if necessary
Use of ICT	• development of keyboard skills • program knowledge • use of word processing • use of spreadsheets, etc.

Subject	Skill areas to develop
Specific text work	• note taking strategies, e.g. main points, abbreviations, personal shorthand
	• comprehension of key information and terminology on the board
	• comprehension of highlighting, underlining, and clear notes from own readability level
	• strategy of Survey, Question, Read, Recall, Review (SQ3R) (see page 31)
	• strategy of Directed Activities Related to Text (DARTS) (see page 32)

While the above may be relevant for other pupils, dyslexic pupils will need to be given more specific help in all these areas.

Mind maps	• ongoing developmental process
	• strategy of mapping
	• focus on key points, branching and associations
	• talking through and tracing with fingers the thinking behind the key points
	• responses from the use of co-operative approaches, prompting questions to develop thinking
	• swapping ideas with others in the group (listener and partner)

See Figure 3 (page 57) and Appendices 9 (Books and resources) and 10 (Useful addresses) for more information on mind mapping.

Homework

Dyslexic pupils will need strategies for homework in order to:

- remember what they have to do;
- remember when it is to be finished and handed in.

Schools need to consider the following points:

- How will they ensure the pupil and parents know what homework is expected and when it is to be completed?
- Will the parents know how to help their child if necessary?
- Will there be time at the end of a session for slow writers to write down their homework?
- What alternative ways are there to ensure homework is known?
- Will the dyslexic pupil benefit from a homework club (if one is available)?
- Does the teacher (subject or general) know the effort that will be needed to complete written assignments?
- Will focus be placed on the 'content' of the homework?
- Can steps be taken to avoid several pieces of homework being given and returned at the same time?
- Is homework negotiated with pupil and parents?
- Is Dyslexia Institute 'homework' also expected?
- Is the pupil engaged in other, valuable after-school activities which are important to him/her?

While these may be common problems, they still need addressing. Answers may be different at different ages and stages of schooling.

In secondary school, homework diaries are common and useful, but are they appropriate if the student cannot write the homework down in time? Reading and spelling activities are common primary school expectations, but can parents help in these activities?

Approaches may be identified whereby:

- a photocopy of the homework is put in the homework diary or exercise book;
- parents have an idea of the homework level at the beginning of each academic year;
- at earlier Key Stages, homework should be negotiated with parents as more specific intervention may be useful;
- strategies for developing phonic knowledge may be done in school and practised at home; school needs to liaise and share with parents how this is done;
- reading approaches and the sharing of reading need to be discussed with parents;

- pupils can be shown how to learn spellings independently, through such methods as Simultaneous Oral Spelling (SOS), Look, Say, Cover, Write, Check (LSCWC) and Read, Remember, Write (RRW);
- spellings may range from learning a letter to a whole word;
- spellings should be within the dyslexic pupil's working memory; this should be identified and words given of 2, 3, 4, 5 or 6 letters in length, given appropriately;
- spellings may also be grouped into rhyming words, phoneme words or irregular words;
- subject-specific spellings are linked with definitions;
- support is given on written work, if needed, in areas of facts, sequence and acknowledgement of slow writing speed/presentation;
- homework levels are monitored and reduced if needed;
- students understand what they have to do; discussions with students will be of benefit.

Study skills

Study skills need teaching and practising. There is no right or wrong way to study but some basic ideas will help. It is important that students know their strengths and weaknesses. The ideas suggested here are by no means definitive and books to support study skills are available.

For dyslexic pupils, studying will be made easier if information has been given in a variety of ways and students have been allowed to record the 'main points' of information.

Dyslexic pupils do not need to be 'overburdened' with a lot of unnecessary information and reading, if mind maps, flow charts and diagrams have been used in initial teaching and learning. Focus should be on highlighting, overlearning and forming the main points of the text.

Drinking water, regular breaks and overlearning should be encouraged. Revising with a friend (non-dyslexic) can also be useful.

Subject teachers need to:
- ensure that students know the type of answers the test requires, e.g. tick boxes, multi-choice, diagram labelling, one-word answers, paragraphs, essays;
- spend time on analysing titles, instructions and questions;
- encourage students to look for textual changes of view with specific vocabulary, e.g.:
  - **but** – changes the point of view;
  - **however** – shows obstacle, changes viewpoint;
  - **whereas** – identifies comparisons;
  - **how** – gives examples, instructions;
- ensure students know how to construct a mind map, and when and how it can be useful;
- use resources such as highlighters for areas that need to stand out in text; for books that cannot be highlighted, Snowpake™ produce repositional adhesive highlighting tabs;
- use Post-its™ – for notes, sequenced information that may need to be rearranged, covering of details for learning and recall.

Check students can use:
- flow charts (show logical progression);
- diagrams and pictures to illustrate main points;
- mind maps.

Auditory learners will benefit from dictating information, listening to tapes and Language Masters, and reading aloud.

Ensure via teaching that students develop thinking and reasoning skills and have developed metacognitive strategies.

Both visual and auditory learners will benefit from ICT with text to speech or speech to text facilities.

Organisation

In terms of organisation, the use of weekly planners will help remind pupils what has to be done and when. Encouragement and help from both teachers and parents should be given in creating a study timetable when homework and revision is needed.

While the decoding and reading of subject-specific words can be achieved, the definitions of such words also need to be learned. Index cards arranged alphabetically can be useful prompts. These should be built up over a period of time. Examples may include:

Photosynthesis	**Science**
(photo-syn-the-sis)	Life processes
(foto-sin-the-sis)*	

a process in which the plant uses sunlight to change/convert water and carbon dioxide into food (starch and sugar)

Subjects could be colour coded.
*Words can be broken down into syllables and spelt phonetically if this is useful.

Encouraging note keeping and the keeping of a notebook to hand will help to record ideas before they are forgotten.

Figures 2, 3 and 4 overleaf illustrate how the above information can be presented to a student in different formats. This may be easier for some students to access.

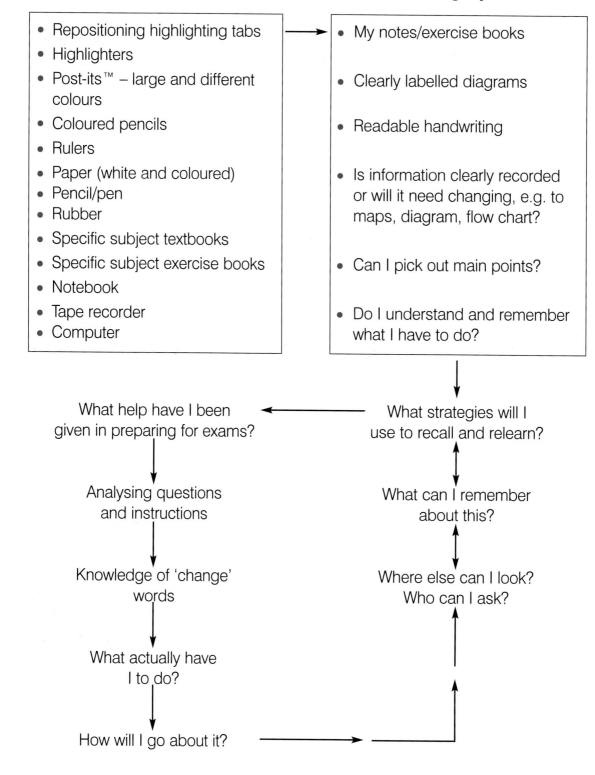

Figure 2 Overview of study skills: organisational checklist

Mind maps

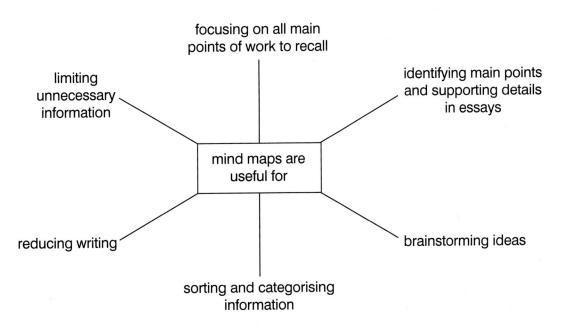

In order to avoid repetition when writing, show students how to pull ideas together in conclusions. It will help to number branches; this will structure the order in which information will be written up or orally discussed. Tick off or blank out those that have been used.

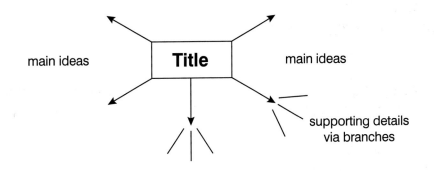

Note: A flow chart could also be used in a similar way, one idea leading to another (see Figure 4).

Figure 3 Recording ideas using mind maps and flow charts: introduction/overview of ideas

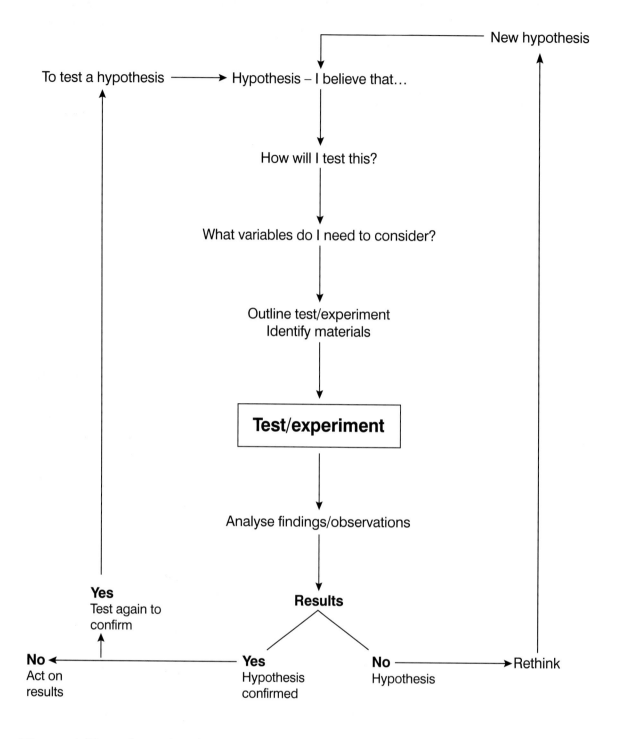

Figure 4 Flow chart showing sequential actions

Statutory assessments and exam concessions

Within the Standard National Tests (Key Stages 1–3), special arrangements can be made for pupils:

- 25% additional time can be given for written tests.
- No permission is needed if tests are separated into sections (time remains the same).
- Pupils can have rest breaks (KS2–3) but must not discuss the test.
- No permission is needed to make taped versions of written tests (KS2–3). (This approach will need practice runs.)
- English cannot be taped.
- No permission is needed if tests are photocopied onto coloured paper or if coloured overlays are used (KS2–3).
- Diagrams can be enhanced (but not changed) (KS2–3). They can be enlarged, cut out, embossed or mounted on card. Bold lines can be added for pupils with spatial difficulties.
- No permission is needed in maths and science if teachers want to provide real objects that look like those illustrated in the text. (Counters cannot be used.)
- Mirrors and tracings can be used at KS3 for symmetry.
- In science apparatus can be 'shown' to pupils.
- Word processors can be used in all tests except English handwriting.
- Spellcheckers cannot be used except for maths/science KS2.
- Dictionaries can be used in all areas except English reading, spelling or extension tests.
- No permission is needed for readers in maths and science unless this leads to a request for extra time.
- No permission is needed for an amanuensis in English, maths and science unless this leads to additional time. (Amanuenses cannot be used for handwriting and only under special circumstances in KS2 for English writing and Level 6 extension.)

Further information can be found in Qualifications and Curriculum Authority (QCA) assessment documentation, produced annually. The information was accurate at the time of printing.

Disapplication

Pupils may be disapplied temporarily or permanently from tests or tasks. However, there are set procedures that the head teacher must follow; these include discussion with parents. If the parent agrees, a 'special direction' will have to be written (copies to pupils' records, chair of governors and the LEA). Parents may change their minds and appeal. The LEA may also not be in favour of disapplication.

The route to disapplication may be through:

- Section 364 of the Education Act (1996); this specifies that some or all of the National Curriculum may be modified or disapplied by a pupil's Statement of SEN.

- Section 365 of the Education Act (1996); this specifies that some or all of the National Curriculum may be temporarily disapplied for a pupil.

Exam concessions for Key Stage 3–4 pupils

In fulfilling required criteria dyslexic pupils can obtain exam concessions. These will be determined via psychological intervention or assessments by staff who have a particular recognised qualification in the teaching of dyslexic pupils.

Additional or amended information can be found in the Joint Council for General Qualifications document: Examinations & Assessment for GCSE & GCE, Stewart House, 32 Russell Square, London, WC1B 5DN

Home–school liaison

Parents hold key information and have a crucial role to play in their children's education. In order to create a good relationship the following suggestions may be helpful:

- Parents should be aware of the Code of Practice and its implications for them.
- Parents should have an understanding of the support stages within the Code and know which stage their child has reached.
- Parents should be invited to contribute to Individual Education Plans (IEPs), attend review meetings and discuss how they can support the IEP.
- Parents should be provided with reports before reviews and/or annual reviews if appropriate.
- Parents should know who to contact if they have concerns about their child, e.g.:
  - Class teacher
  - SENCO
  - Head teacher
  - Special needs governor.
- Parental concerns should be listened to and acknowledged. A family history can be useful as dyslexia can be genetic, particularly on the male side.
- Parents should be trusted as partners.
- Parents may be encouraged to become involved in the life of the school, e.g. as reading partners, helpers on school trips.
- Ensure parents are informed of visits from other professionals, e.g. educational psychologist, teachers who have qualifications in dyslexia.
- Consult parents before changes in provision are made.
- Use a home/school diary to allow school and home to create a dialogue about what the child is doing.
- Celebrate success, large or small, with parents.
- Give parents ideas and strategies to help with learning at home – link with games.
- Give suggestions for games and activities which can help areas such as co-ordination, motor skills, memory and sequencing.
- If parents have problems/fears in approaches to or by the school, especially by letter, alternative means of communication may be needed.
- 'Show' parents how they can help, rather than just explain.

If students have any 'specialist teaching', it may be useful to see if parents could attend a session and/or discuss matters with the specialist.

Support staff: roles and responsibilities

Support staff should:

have a clear understanding of their roles and responsibilities:

- Have a knowledge of their job description.
- Know that information given to parents should be with the knowledge of the class teacher.
- Respect the confidentiality of information about pupils.
- Maintain a professional demeanour with parents.
- Be aware of school policies with regard to behaviour, anti-bullying, Child Protection, etc.

be aware of the channels of communication within school:

- Ensure that information given by parents is relayed to the SENCO/class teacher/form tutor.
- Ensure that communication with outside agencies is carried out in consultation with the SENCO.
- Ensure that there is a mechanism for disseminating information to support staff about school activities, e.g. day book, staff room, noticeboard.

be recognised as valued team members:

- Participate in the planning and monitoring process.
- Celebrate and share their expertise.

be encouraged to make use of their personal skills:

- Share skills in the areas of ICT, organisation, creative arts.

be supported with appropriate, ongoing professional development opportunities:

- Observe and learn from other professionals.
- Take advantage of training opportunities in school and relevant external courses.

encourage pupils' independence at all times:

- Promote independent work habits.
- Promote independent life skills.
- Promote independent play skills.

Support staff: effective deployment

Not all pupils with dyslexia will require additional adult support in order to meet their needs within the classroom. For those pupils who have a more significant level of need, however, the provision of support staff is vital to ensure that their needs can be met.

Teachers may consider the following issues to ensure the most effective deployment of support staff:

- Support staff should promote independence at all times.
- It will not be necessary to work alongside the pupil in every lesson.
- Consider the position of support staff within the classroom.
- Allow the pupil to focus on the teacher, rather than on support staff.
- Support staff should take notes during teacher input in order to reinforce key points at a later stage in the lesson.
- Support staff should monitor and record appropriate information about the pupil, e.g. work output, temperament.
- Liaison procedures between home and school should be established under the guidance of the SENCO/head of year/class teacher or form tutor.
- Support staff should work under the direction of the SENCO, class teacher or individual subject teachers.
- In practical sessions when the pupil needs to manipulate specialised equipment, support staff should work under the direction of the pupil.
- Withdrawal of the pupil for dyslexia programmes should be negotiated with the SENCO and individual subject teachers.

> The ultimate responsibility for a pupil's access to the curriculum is that of the classroom teacher. Support staff facilitate the delivery of an appropriate differentiated curriculum under the direction of the teacher.

Support assistant as facilitator

The role of the support assistant is to help pupils access the curriculum. The role may encompass the following:

1. **Translator:** Translates information into diagrammatic formats or in any manner that aids understanding/recall.

2. **Interpreter:** Explains complex points; isolates main points, i.e. complex to straightforward.

3. **Scribe:** Helps with précis and note taking. Identifies main points. Length and detail will vary, depending on child and subject.

4. **Memory jogger:**

   M
   - where and why
   - equipment
   - recall of last lesson
   - homework

5. **Questioner:** Where? What? Why? When? How?

   understanding

   recall strategies

   meaning

6. **Focuser:** Look at that…
   Check that number, letter, answer.
   What should sentences begin with…?
   Listen to…

7. **Tactician:** Flexible ways of operating. Being sensitive and aware.

8. **Diplomat:** Within situations and with individuals. Between pupil, home and school.

9. **Encourager:** Helps build up confidence and foster positive attitudes.

10. **Listener:** Within formal situations. As a 'friend' in informal situations if wanted.

11. **Do-er:** Models and demonstrates (positive behaviours and the 'how' of learning).

12. **Enabler:**

    E

    How did you say you would remember?

    Remember when…

    This is how…

Individual Education Plans

An Individual Education Plan (IEP) should focus ideally on a specific area or target which the pupil will work on (and achieve) over a realistic period of time. They are designed specifically for pupils who have additional or special needs and are implemented at school level, via School Action or School Action Plus, which involves outside agencies and forms part of the graduated level of identified need and support. Learning objectives and strategies which form part of the pupil's normal classroom practice do not form part of the IEP.

IEPs are usually made up of 'smart' targets or objectives. Such targets are:

Simple
Measurable
Achievable
Relevant
Timed

Some targets may be more general in nature. This will be more evident where pupils are involved in the target-setting process, something that is advocated by OFSTED and the SEN Code of Practice.

Targets within IEPs may be levelled against National Curriculum P Scales and sub-levels but most dyslexia targets cannot be levelled in the same way. (See examples on pages 68 and 70)

The review process should look at what the pupil has achieved. Appropriate teaching will have ensured consistency and accuracy in the pupil's outcomes.

The dyslexic pupil

The dyslexic pupil may be working from a published multi-sensory programme at School Action or School Action Plus. A structured teaching programme, usually of an hour's duration, is usually based on a multi-sensory approach involving:

- Organisational skills
- Sequencing
- Auditory and visual memory
- Syllable work
- Blending
- Recall (reading and spelling phonemes)
- New teaching point (phoneme)
- Auditory and visual discrimination
- Handwriting
- Dictation
- Spelling

Teachers trained specifically to use multi-sensory programmes or who have qualifications to teach dyslexic pupils may work through such programmes and these will act as or form part of an IEP.

An IEP may need to cover additional areas of weakness. Pupils should learn through their strengths with areas of weakness being approached in such a way that skills and strategies are developed in these areas.

Example Individual Education Plans

Primary pupil: Example

David is a Year 4 pupil who has ongoing problems with literacy. He is quite vocal in class and will recall some but not all the information he has heard. When given prompts or picture clues his responses are more accurate. He appears 'bright' but isn't making the expected progress. He enjoys stories but dislikes reading and is reluctant to try.

Problems include:

- hearing medial vowels;
- identifying rhyme (auditory);
- segmenting words and isolating sounds;
- blending phonemes;
- recalling words;
- using strategies in reading;
- spelling does not reflect phonemic knowledge;
- vowels are sometimes missed out and he has problems with v/th/f.

His handwriting is poor and he wants to work on this; some of this will be addressed in school and via the school writing scheme Nelson, but he also needs practice in joining and with diagonal lines. Writing generally lacks control.

He has had support at School Action in additional reading and spelling, but is still not making the expected progress. The school needs additional strategies and ideas. Parents are concerned and are willing to help. Assessments show:

- alphabet knowledge:
  - $\frac{10}{26}$ letter names;
  - $\frac{18}{26}$ letter sounds;
- problems matching upper- and lower-case letters;
- he can read 41, Reception high frequency words;
- he can spell 22, Reception high frequency words;
- work (teacher assessment) at Level 1b in reading and spelling;
- work between 2c and b, depending on the subject, in speaking and listening;
- good social skills but problems with independence and organisation (elements P6–9);
- attention P10.

Within the IEP 3–4 areas will be focused on, with other areas covered within the management and teaching of the class. He has been referred to an outside agency for support.

Class work is to be differentiated with an emphasis on visually presented materials.

Primary school

Name: David		DOB:	School Action/School Action Plus

IEP date: September 03   **NC Year:** 4   **Review date:** December 03

Nature of difficulties: Dyslexia
Memory (auditory)
Recall and use of Year 1/2 high frequency words
Reluctant reader. Problems sequencing and saying alphabet

Strengths:
Stronger visual memory
Good at identifying rhyme visually
He is keen to learn

Targets	Strategies	Resources	Evaluation
To follow structured teaching programmes Teaching Points 1–10	Multi-sensory approaches as per the programme Home to support reading and spelling packs Liaison with school to inform staff as to needs of dyslexic pupils	Dyslexia Literacy Programme (Dlp) – trained teacher in (Spld) dyslexia (outside agency to deliver programme) Resources supplied by agency	
To recall series of random letters in correct sequence and orientation Increase letters from 4 to 7 **Aim: To use process to learn high frequency words (4–7 in length) when the above is achieved**	Auditory and visual approaches Gradually increase number of letters presented Letter names used. Alphabet placed in arc shape Visual – pupil to look for 5 seconds, scan and touch alphabet letters Pull out recalled letters Auditory – teacher to say names; pupil repeats and pulls letters from arc To do minimum 3 times a week	Wooden letters Auditory and visual letter cards Large table Outside agency Learning support assistant (LSA)	
To sequence the alphabet, name letters in and out of sequence Say and write the alphabet	Organise wooden letters prior to setting out Put letters out in groups if helpful: A...G H..K L...P Q...U V...Z Learn in chunks. Sing and place letters if helpful. Say letter names as placed/written To do daily with/without support	Wooden letters Large table Prompt cards Alphabet cassette tape if helpful	
Pupil target To use letters correctly when writing	Tracing using haptic memory, air writing using kinaesthetic memory, copy work	Sandpaper letters	
Parental support	Practise reading and spelling packs daily Learn 'paired reading' strategies and use 3 times a week to support David reading from the school reading scheme	New Way Reading Scheme	

Secondary pupil

Jim is a Year 8 pupil who was identified as having problems in reading, writing and organisational skills.

He had support from his primary school at School Action, but there were concerns from both the school and parents as to the possibility of dyslexia. It was confirmed that the father had significant literacy problems when at school and still finds reading and writing difficult.

Jim left primary school with:

- Level 5 in science)
- Level 4 in maths) having a reader in both subjects
- Below Level 3 in literacy (although it was felt he was just a Level 3 by the school in reading and writing and Level 4 in speaking)

In Year 7 he was assessed by a teacher trained to teach dyslexic pupils and he began a Dyslexia Literacy Programme (Dlp) which he responded to well, covering 34 Teaching Points. This increased his confidence, and use of phonemic skills.

He is keen to learn in a one-to-one situation, but he has very poor self-esteem when in a group. Most of the focused support is in withdrawal sessions with a specialist teacher. There is support assistant liaison to aid transfer of skills and strategies to class and independent work.

His memory skills when working on auditory and visual techniques are much improved. He can now recall nine letters consistently in both modalities but needs to transfer these skills into formal language work.

Advice to schools

To aid access to curriculum studies it will be beneficial to transfer these techniques to develop subject-specific vocabulary from selected NC KS3 schemes of work.

In the learning situation information should be presented as key points. Information should also be presented via worksheets, and encouraged use of highlighters and oral responses will help him to internalise key points of information. He finds working at home difficult and most support will need to be made by the school. He should not be expected to copy work from a distance.

Secondary school

Name: Jim	DOB:		School Action/School Action Plus

IEP date: January 03   **NC Year:** 8   **Review date:** March 03

Nature of difficulties: Dyslexia
Organisational skills
Reading age 9.7. Problems in recall and structuring ideas for writing

Strengths:
Good recall of letters in short-term memory (9)
Following Dyslexia Institute literacy programme successfully

Targets	Strategies	Resources	Evaluation
To follow structured teaching programmes Teaching Points 35–45	Withdrawal one hour weekly Multi-sensory approaches to learning Teaching assistant to liaise with specialist teacher re follow-up work	Dyslexia Literacy Programme (Dlp) delivered by outside agency, dyslexia trained teacher Resources supplied by agency	
To read and spell subject-specific words for current term: Science History	Use auditory and visual memory approaches as in above programme Syllable division Read, Remember, Write (RRW) Simultaneous Oral Spelling (SOS) ICT work Link with definitions	List of vocabulary from Science National Curriculum documents, *8d ecological relationships Trained teacher (dyslexia) and LSA History Unit 8 Industrial Changes Starspell Workshark Language Master	
To structure ideas prior to writing	Develop brainstorming and mind mapping techniques Recall previous information via questions and prompts Look at flow diagrams and compare with mind mapping	Information from English and/or history department as to current programmes of study Examples of mind mapping and flow diagram Visual material to use as a basis for writing Use of ICT/trained teacher/LSA	

Are you a dyslexia-friendly school?

	Yes	No
Is dyslexia status recognised by the school?	☐	☐
Are the governors and senior managers committed to supporting dyslexic pupils across the whole curriculum?	☐	☐
Are issues related to dyslexia identified within the School Improvement Plan?	☐	☐
Do all staff recognise the strengths and weaknesses of dyslexic pupils and teach accordingly?	☐	☐
Is training provided for all staff as an ongoing developmental process?	☐	☐
Do dyslexic pupils have access to 1:1 teaching by a teacher with a dyslexia qualification or trained to teach dyslexic pupils?	☐	☐
Does the school have access to support systems that have specially trained teachers and resources?	☐	☐
Has the school appropriate materials for teaching dyslexic pupils?	☐	☐
Are dyslexic pupils given appropriate work for their ability levels?	☐	☐
Does the school encourage effective parent partnerships?	☐	☐
Do policies such as marking, assessment, homework, behaviour and Personal, Social and Health Education (PSHE) support the dyslexic pupil?	☐	☐
Have dyslexic pupils appropriate Individual Education Plans (IEPs)?	☐	☐
Is the pupil involved in the IEP and/or support plan?	☐	☐

	Yes	No
Are pupils given the confidence and necessary emotional support?	☐	☐
Are pupils encouraged to go into Further Education?	☐	☐
Does the school endeavour to talk to parents and obtain family histories?	☐	☐
If a pupil attends the Dyslexia Institute, does the school liaise with the institute?	☐	☐
Are classrooms dyslexia-friendly? e.g.:	☐	☐

Are classrooms dyslexia-friendly? e.g.:

- supportive to dyslexic pupils;
- providing appropriate teaching, e.g. mnemonics, tables, mind maps, timetables, homework boards, lesson prompts, subject-specific and definition information booklets.

The responses to these questions may be used as the basis for an action plan.

Where 'yes' is identified, is there evidence to support this? If not, can this be gathered or identified?

Where 'no' is identified, what action will be taken and in what priority?

Similarities between dyslexia and dyspraxia

- Late development of speech
- Difficulties with speech
- Problems with self-dressing
- Confused laterality
- Forgetful/memory problems
- Difficulties following instructions/directions
- Poor sense of direction
- Problems with orientation
- Problems with sequencing
- Poor organisation/untidy
- Poor processing of verbal information
- Sometimes clumsy
- Difficulties copying from blackboard
- Odd pencil grip
- Poor handwriting
- Difficulties getting it down on paper
- Inconsistent school performance
- Difficulties paying attention
- Anxiety
- Sensitivity
- Low self-esteem

(Dyslexia Handbook 2001: Double Diagnosis or Development Diversity (Gail Goedkoop))

Contrasts between dyslexia and dyspraxia

Dyslexia

- Early or normal motor milestones
- Performance IQ > Verbal IQ (often greater)
- Often good at sports
- Strengths in art and craft skills
- Often strong in personal skills
- Usually reading problems
- Problems with word finding, rhymes, phonological awareness
- Always spelling problems
- Often good at maths concepts
- More often genetic history

Dyspraxia

- Late motor development
- Weak posture and muscle tone
- Verbal IQ > Performance IQ (almost always greater verbally)
- Poor gross motor skills, poor at PE
- Poor fine motor skills, dislike of crafts and art
- Difficulties with social skills
- Usually no reading difficulties unless visual reading problems
- More writing than spelling difficulties
- Weak at maths concepts
- More likely a difficult birth history

(Dyslexia Handbook 2001: Double Diagnosis or Development Diversity (Gail Goedkoop))

Characteristics of a dyslexic pupil

We have all come across the situation. A child who is struggling with spelling, writing or reading, or perhaps numeracy. A child who does not progress as quickly as his/her classmates – or worse, does not seem to progress at all. And yet there are obvious inconsistencies because the child achieves well in other areas.

You think the child will improve in time – but you see no change. Then someone mentions dyslexia, and you start to wonder. But you tell yourself that children often get over such early difficulties, and you hope for the best. Yet you still feel uneasy. This child is different.

So how *do* you tell if a child may be dyslexic? There are some obvious signs, if you know what to look for. But not all children have the same cluster of *abilities* or *difficulties*.

Look out for the following areas of weakness:

General:
- processing of spoken and/or written language is slow;
- has poor concentration;
- has difficulty following instructions;
- is forgetful of words.

Written work:
- has poor standard of written work compared with oral ability;
- produces messy work with many crossings out and words tried several times, e.g. 'wippe', 'wype', 'wiep', 'wipe';
- is persistently confused by letters that look similar, particularly b/d, p/g, p/q, n/u, m/w;
- has poor handwriting, with many reversals and badly formed letters;
- spells a word several different ways in one piece of writing;
- makes anagrams of words, e.g. 'tired' for 'tried', 'breaded' for 'bearded';
- produces badly set-out written work, doesn't stay close to the margin;
- has poor pencil grip;
- produces phonetic and bizarre spellings; not age/ability-appropriate;
- uses unusual sequences of letters or words.

Reading:
- makes slow progress with reading, especially using look-and-say methods;
- finds it difficult to blend letters together;
- has difficulty in establishing syllable division or knowing the beginnings or endings of words;

- pronunciation of words is unusual;
- has no expression in reading; comprehension poor;
- is hesitant in reading, especially when reading aloud;
- misses out words when reading, or adds extra words;
- fails to recognise familiar words;
- loses the point of a story being read or written;
- has difficulty in picking out the most important points from a passage.

Numeracy:
- shows confusion with number order, e.g. units, tens, hundreds;
- is confused by symbols, e.g. + and × signs;
- has difficulty with sequential order, e.g. tables, days of the week, the alphabet.

Time:
- has difficulty in learning to tell the time;
- shows poor time keeping and general awareness;
- has poor personal organisation;
- has difficulty in remembering his/her birth date, what day of the week it is, month of the year, seasons of the year;
- has difficulty with concepts, e.g. yesterday, today, tomorrow.

Skills:
- has poor motor skills: weaknesses in speed, control and accuracy with a pencil;
- has a limited understanding of non-verbal communication;
- is confused by the difference between left and right, up and down, east and west;
- has indeterminate hand preference;
- performs unevenly from day to day.

Behaviour:
- employs work avoidance tactics, such as sharpening pencils and looking for books;
- seems to 'dream', does not seem to listen;
- is easily distracted;
- is the class clown, or is disruptive or withdrawn (these are often cries for help);
- is excessively tired, due to the amount of concentration and effort required.

A child who has a cluster of these difficulties together with some abilities may be dyslexic.

Your next step should be to consult the school's SENCO immediately, and to decide whether the parents should be informed and the child given appropriate help. (DfES 2001, in association with BDA publication Achieving Dyslexia Friendly Schools).

Assessments

Ongoing teacher assessments are valuable sources of information as is the teacher knowledge of the pupil and his/her working profile.

Within assessments, miscue analysis (looking for the types of mistakes and analysing them) will help identify gaps and areas to focus on.

While observable behaviours give strong indicators of possible dyslexia, assessments may be carried out by professionals which will provide more precise information with profiles of intelligence, strengths and weaknesses.

Assessments may be done by educational psychologists, specialist teachers, support services and institutes. Some tests such as Wechsler Intelligence Scales for Children (WISC) can only be given by psychologists, but there are a growing number of tests available from the Psychological Corporation that can be done in schools.

The most commonly used tests by specialist teachers continue to be:

- Aston Index Assessment (5–14 years)
- Bangor
- British Picture Vocabulary Scale (BPVS) (receptive language)
- Dyslexia Early Screening Test (DEST) (4.6–6.5 years)
- Dyslexia Screening Test (DST) (6.6–16.5 years)
- Phonological Abilities Test (PAT) (4–7 years)
- Phonological Assessment Battery (PhAb) (6–14.11 years)

Non-Verbal Reasoning Tests are sometimes used, as are computerised systems such as the Cognitive Profiling System (CoPs) for primary schools and Lucid Assessment System (LASS) for secondary schools. The Dyslexia Adult Test (DAST) assesses those of 16.6 years and above.

It is important to stress that it is in the interpretation of such information and the appropriate programmes and strategies put in place, where assessment skills are needed.

N.B. This information is correct at the time of publication. However, tests are revised so correct catalogue information should be checked.

Visual dyslexia

Up to 5 years, children may:

- encounter problems with sunshine;
- have sore eyes;
- squint;
- have lazy eye/reduced acuity;
- experience frontal headaches;
- be prone to allergies/asthma, etc.;
- be hyperactive;
- suffer from Attention Deficit Disorder (ADD).

5 to 8 years, in addition to the above, children may:

- experience difficulty learning to read;
- have concentration problems;
- attempt to reduce light levels;
- rub their eyes frequently when reading;
- develop red eyes when reading;
- reverse words/letters when reading;
- experience difficulty with reading the ends of words (e.g. will guess at the end of simple words such as 'there', 'that', etc.);
- re-read or skip lines;
- miss words out;
- experience a reduction in self-esteem.

9 to 12 years, in addition to the above, children may:

- experience pattern glare;
- begin falling behind their peers at school;
- behave disruptively;
- be reluctant to read.

12 to 16 years, in addition to the above, children may:

- experience increased pattern glare;
- experience low self-esteem, possibly leading to depression;
- experience migraines.

(Visual Dyslexia: A Guide for Parents and Teachers (Ian Jordan))

Skills development

Teachers need to ensure that pupils are supported in developing both thinking and key skills via explanations, practice and encouragement.

The National Curriculum 2000 Key Stages 1 and 2	
Thinking skills Knowing how – learning how to learn	**Key skills** Learning to improve learning and performance in education, work and life
Information-processing skills: These enable pupils to: • Locate and collect relevant information. • Sort, classify, sequence, and compare and contrast. • Analyse part/whole relationships.	**Communication:** • Speak effectively for different audiences. • Listen, understand and respond to others appropriately, and participate effectively in group discussion. • Read with fluency a range of literacy and non-fiction texts and reflect critically. • Write with fluency for a range of purposes and audiences, including critical analysis of their own and others'.
Reasoning skills: These enable pupils to: • Give reasons for opinions and actions. • Draw references and make deductions. • Use precise language to explain what they think. • Make judgements and decisions informed by reasons and evidence.	**Application of number:** • Use mental calculation skills. • Understand and use mathematical language. • Process data. • Solve increasingly complex number problems and explain reasoning.
Enquiry skills: These enable pupils to: • Ask relevant questions. • Pose and define problems. • Plan what to do and how to research. • Predict outcomes and anticipate consequences. • Test conclusions and improve ideas.	**Information technology:** • Use a range of information sources and ICT tools. • Analyse, interpret, evaluate and present information for a range of purposes. • Make critical and informed judgements about how and when to use ICT. • Use ICT for maximum benefit in accessing information, in solving problems or for expressive work.

Thinking skills Knowing how – learning how to learn	Key skills Learning to improve learning and performance in education, work and life
Creative thinking skills: These enable pupils to: • Generate and extend ideas. • Suggest hypotheses. • Apply imagination. • Look for alternative innovative outcomes.	**Working with others:** • Contribute to small-group and whole-class discussion. • Work with others to meet a challenge. • Develop the social skills to work with others. • Have a growing awareness and understanding of the needs of others. • Work effectively with others in formal and informal settings. • Appreciate the experience of others. • Consider different perspectives and benefit from what others say and do.
Evaluation skills: These enable pupils to: • Evaluate information. • Judge the value of what they read, hear and do. • Develop criteria for judging the value of their own and others' work or ideas. • Have confidence in their judgements.	**Improving own learning and performance:** • Reflect and critically evaluate their own work, what they have learned, and identify ways of improving their own learning and performance. • Be able to identify the purpose of learning. • Reflect on the process of learning, assess progress in learning, identify obstacles to learning and plan ways to improve. **Problem-solving:** • Develop skills and strategies that will help pupils solve the problems they face in learning and in life. • Develop the skills of identifying and understanding a problem, monitor progress in tackling a problem and review solutions to problems.

Legal and operational perspectives

There have been some recent high profile cases about the negligence/breach of statutory duty by teachers and/or psychologists due to their failure to diagnose dyslexia in an individual and, therefore, to address appropriately the special educational needs of this individual. In the case of Phelps v. Hillingdon LBC (House of Lords, 27 July 2000), the House of Lords held that:

"educational pychologists and teachers have a duty of care to ensure that children receive education appropriate to their needs. Even though the authority can not be sued for a direct breach of their statutory duties, it did not follow that the authority could never be vicariously liable for negligent acts by employees in the course of the performance of the duty. Indeed, it was fair, just and reasonable that liability should attach, as the child and parents rely on their advice. The fact that the professionals' direct duty was to the authority does not mean that they do not owe a duty to the child."

Lord Nicholls of Birkenhead emphasised that *"this decision is not to open the door to claims based on poor quality of teaching"* and that there was a world of difference between claims for manifest incompetence and those of a more general nature.

The implications of the above ruling together with the Human Rights Act (2000) and the SEN and Disability Act (2001) (SENDA) are as follows:

- Schools and teachers have a duty to ensure that children receive education appropriate to their needs, irrespective of the nature and extent of those needs and whether or not the need has a diagnostic label (e.g. dyslexia).
- The definition of the working party to the British Psychological Society (1999) provides the basis for a staged approach of assessment through teaching.
- Teachers should maintain records of their work with special needs children including dyslexic pupils in line with the Revised Code of Practice.
- Expert assessments by psychologists or other specialists can help contribute to an understanding of a child's difficulties including those of dyslexic pupils, *but* such assessments need to be part of a comprehensive programme of support organised primarily by the school and its teachers for that child.
- Educational psychologists should, when assessing the special educational needs of children, follow the framework for psychological assessment (1999) and the Division of Educational and Child Psychology (DECP) Guidelines for the Practice of Educational Psychologists (EPs) (1993). This model provides the 'gold' standard by which an individual EP's practice may be judged.

There is a biological involvement in all cases of dyslexia; the biological differences between dyslexics and non-dyslexics may be genetic, acquired or perhaps both. At the cognitive level the prevailing expert opinion is that phonological deficit and delay is central to the difficulties of dyslexic pupils. Other cognitive difficulties contribute to the phonological difficulties or are consequential.

There is an extensive number of symptoms and signs of dyslexia at the behavioural level, the most disabling being that of word decoding and encoding. The existence of severe and persistent difficulties at the word level, despite appropriate learning opportunities, confirms dyslexia. Confirmation of these other difficulties listed at the behavioural level within the identification section of this book offers further diagnostic and supporting evidence of the presence of dyslexia as well as evidence of additional special needs.

Software and websites

- Crick Software
  Tel: 01604 671691
  www.oncksoft.com

  Clicker 4
  All My Words (literacy)
  Word Bar (older secondary pupils)

- iAnsyst Ltd
  72 Fen Road
  Cambridge
  CB4 1GZ
  Freephone: 0500 141515
  Email: sales@dyslexic.com
  www.dyslexia.com

  Information on all Key Stages
  Ranges of products and services
  which use technology to help
  people with dyslexia.
  Trial version of a program
  called Inspiration to do with
  mind mapping can be found at
  www.inspiration.com or
  www.dyslexic.com/inspir.htm

- Leeds & Bradford Dyslexia Association
  Email: jane@labda.org.uk
  www.labda.org.uk

  ICT information

- Listening Books
  (The National Listening Library)
  www.listeningbooks.org.uk

  £50 membership provides postal
  audio library service (general reading,
  GCSE course books, etc.)

- Reading Quest
  curry.edschool.virginia.edu/go/readquest/strat

  Reading comprehension

- SEMERC Information
  Tel: 0161 827 2719
  www.semerc.com

  ICT information for SEN students

- Sight-Sound Technology
  Quantel House, Anglia House
  Moulton Park
  Northampton
  NN3 6JA
  Tel: 01604 798070
  Email: sales@sightandsound.co.uk

  Kurzweil 3000 (scans written pages
  and speaks the text)

- Texthelp Systems Ltd
  Freepost BEL 3628
  Antrim
  BT41 4BR
  Northern Ireland
  www.texthelp.com

  Software that supports and develops literacy
  Type-talk: word processor including Read and Write (speech feedback, Thesaurus, etc.)

- Visual Dyslexia
  www.visualdyslexia.com

  Information on visual dyslexia (Ian Jordan)

- White Space Ltd
  41 Mail Road
  London
  W6 9DG
  www.wordshark.co.uk

  Wordshark
  Numbershark
  Super Starspell

- www.dyscalculia.org/edu503html

Search engine information

- Google (www.google.com) is a useful search engine, containing in excess of 1,000,000 pages and 154,000 references on dyslexia.

To narrow the field of search within the search boxes, type in additional information. Once an area of research has been identified, e.g. if you need to find out about teaching maths in the UK only, the section called Advanced Searches will also give tips on accessing specific areas.

Books and resources

- Achieving Dyslexia Friendly Schools
  Tel: 0118 9662677

  BDA Publications (1999)

- Dyslexia, Dyscalculia and some Remedial
  Perspectives for Mathematics Teaching

  Mahesh C. Sharma

- Dyslexia, Literacy and Psychological
  Assessment

  The British Psychological
  Society (1999)
  ISBN 1 85433 310 0

- Specific Learning Difficulties (Dyslexia):
  A Teacher's Guide

  Margaret Crombie (1991)
  Jordanhill College of Education
  ISBN 1 85098 418 2

- The Dyslexia Handbook 2004
  Tel: 0118 966 2677

  Mike Johnson and
  Lindsay Peer (Eds)
  BDA Publications

- Visual Dyslexia (2000): A Guide for Parents
  and Teachers

  Ian Jordan
  Desktop Publications
  ISBN 1 90271 000 2

- Visual Dyslexia (2000): Signs, Symptoms
  and Assessment

  Ian Jordan
  Desktop Publications
  ISBN 1 90271 025 8

Further books and resources

- Teaching Today Pack: Dyslexia in the
  Primary School (video and booklet)
  BBC Educational Publishing
  PO Box 234
  Wetherby
  West Yorkshire
  LS23 7EU
  (approx £30 + pp)

  BBC (1997)

- The Speed Reading Book

  Tony Buzan (2000)
  BBC Books
  ISBN 0 56353 731 0

- Use Your Head

  Tony Buzan (2003)
  BBC Books
  ISBN 0 56348 899 9

- Practical Strategies for Living with Dyslexia

  Maria Chivers (2001)
  Jessica Kingsley
  ISBN 1 85302 905 X

- Toe by Toe: A Highly Structured Multi-Sensory Reading Manual for Teachers and Parents

  Keda and Harry Cowling (1993)
  K & H Cowling
  ISBN 0 95225 640 1

- The Gift of Dyslexia

  Ronald D Davies (1997)
  Souvenir Press
  ISBN 0 20563 412 7

- Brain Gym

  Paul Dennison (1984)
  Educational Kinesiology
  Foundation
  ISBN 0 94214 302 7

- Specific Difficulties in Mathematics: A Classroom Approach

  Olwen El-Naggar (1996)
  Nasen Publications
  ISBN 0 90673 081 3

- Dyslexia in Focus at 16 Plus: An Inclusive Teaching Approach

  Jeanne Holloway (2000)
  Nasen Publications
  ISBN 1 90148 519 6

- Thinking Skills to Thinking Classroom

  Carol McGuiness (1999)
  DFEE Review Report

- Identifying and Supporting Skills in the Dyslexic Child
  Tel: 01652 688781

  Carol Mellers (1993)
  Desktop Publications
  ISBN 1 87240 636 X

- Making Your Secondary Classroom Dyslexia Friendly
  Tel: 01652 656552

  Kate Moore (1998)
  Desktop Publications
  ISBN 1 87240 695 5

- Ace Dictionary
  Aurally Coded English (phonic aural identification to correct spelling)

  David Moseley (1995)
  LDA Publications
  ISBN 1 85503 214 7

- TakeTime: Movement Exercises for Parents, Teachers and Therapists of Children with Difficulties in Speaking, Reading, Writing and Spelling

  Mary Nash-Wortham (1994)
  Robinswood Press
  ISBN 1 86998 150 2

- How to Detect and Manage Dyslexia

  Philomena Ott (1997)
  BDA Publications
  ISBN 0 43510 419 5

- The National Numeracy Strategy: Guidance to Support Pupils with Specific Needs in the Daily Mathematics
  Tel: 0845 60 222 60

  QCA
  Ref: DfES 1545/2001

- Helping Children Cope with Dyslexia

  Sally Raymond (2000)
  Sheldon Press
  ISBN 0 85969 875 0

- Move It: Physical Movement and Learning
  Network Educational Press Ltd
  PO Box 635
  Stafford
  ST16 1BF

  Alistair Smith (2002)
  Network Educational Press
  ISBN 1 85539 123 6

- Working with Children with Specific Learning Difficulties in the Early Years

  Dorothy Smith (2001)
  QEd
  ISBN 1 89887 368 6

- Individual Education Plans: Dyslexia

  Janet Tod (2000)
  David Fulton
  ISBN 1 85346 523 2

- Dyslexia: A Staff Development Handbook

  Colin Tyre (1998)
  QEd
  ISBN 1 89887 306 2

- Dyslexia and Vision

  Bruce Evans (2003)
  Whurr Publishers
  ISBN 1 86156 242 X

Useful addresses

- Basic Skills Agency (Literacy and Numeracy) Tel: 020 7405 4017
  Commonwealth House
  1–19 New Oxford Street
  London WC1A 1NU

- British Association of Behavioural Optometrists Tel: 01277 624916
  c/o Aquila Optometrists
  72 High Street
  Billericay
  Essex CM12 9BS

- British Association of Behavioural Optometrists Tel: 01242 602 689
  c/o Christine Manser
  Greygarth, Littleworth
  Winchcombe
  Cheltenham GL54 5BT
  www.babo.co.uk

- British Dyslexia Association (BDA) Tel: 0118 966 8271
  98 London Road
  Reading RG1 5AU
  www.bda-dyslexia.org.uk

- CreSTeD The Council for the
  Christine Manser – Administrator Registration of Schools
  Grey Garth Teaching Dyslexic Pupils
  Littleworth Tel: 01242 602689
  Winchcombe
  Cheltenham GL54 5BT

- Desktop Publications For a variety of publications
  54 Railway Street on dyslexia
  Barnety-le-Wold Tel: 01652 656552
  North Lincolnshire DN38 6DQ
  www.desktoppublications.co.uk

- Developmental Practitioners' Association Focus on early developmental
  PO Box 4567 reflexes which may need
  Henley on Thames stimulating – neuro-developmental
  Oxfordshire RG9 6XZ therapy

- Dyslexia, Dyspraxia and Attention Disorders
  Treatment Centre (DDAT)
  6 The Square
  Kenilworth
  Warwickshire CV8 1EB
  www.ddat.org

  Tel: 0845 025 0550

- Educational Kinesiology Foundation
  12 Golders Rise
  London NW4 2HR

  Body Balance, Brain Gym
  associated materials
  Tel: 020 8202 9747

- Hornsby International Dyslexia Centre
  Wye Street
  London SE11 2HB
  Email: dyslexia@hornsby.co.uk
  www.hornsby.co.uk

  New developments and courses
  Tel: 020 7223 1144

- Institute of Optometry
  56–62 Newington Causeway
  London SE1 6DS

  Tel: 020 7234 9641

- Joint Council for General Qualifications
  Stewart House
  32 Russell Square
  London WC1B 5DN
  Email: jointcouncil@edexcel.org.uk

  Tel: 0870 240 9800

- Keywords
  Copies of Keywords
  Basic Skills Agency
  P.O. Box 270
  Wetherby
  West Yorks LS23 7BJ

  Semi-blank dictionary, in which
  to put subject-specific words,
  their definitions and alternative
  word choices, e.g. plus/add/
  increase
  Tel: 0870 600 2400

- LDA Catalogue
  Duke St
  Wisbech
  Cambridgeshire PE13 2AE

  Beat Dyslexia and other resources
  Alpha to Omega and other
  resources
  Tel: 01945 463441

- Lucid Research Ltd
  3 Spencer Street, Beverley
  East Yorks HU17 9EG

  CoPs LASS Assessments
  Tel: 01482 465589

- Multi-Sensory Learning Ltd
  Highgate House
  Creaton
  Northamptonshire NN6 8NN

  Multi-Sensory Learning/
  Structured Literacy Programme
  and others
  Tel: 01536 399002

- Nasen Publications
  Nasen House
  4/5 Amber Business Village
  Amber Close
  Tamworth
  Staffordshire B77 4RF
  www.nasen.org.uk

- PATOSS
  PO Box 10
  Evesham
  Worcestershire WR11 1ZW
  Email; patoss@evesham.ac.uk
  www.patoss-dyslexia.org

  Professional Association of
  Teachers of Students with Specific
  Learning Difficulties e.g. Spid.
  dyslexia, dyspraxia, ADD,
  Asperger's syndrome

- Psychological Corporation
  Harcourt Place
  21 Jamestown Road
  London NW1 1YA
  Email: tpc@harcourt.com
  www.tpc-international.com

  For a variety of assessment
  materials e.g. Dyslexia Early
  Screening Test (DEST), Dyslexia
  Screening Test (DST)
  Tel: 020 7424 4456

- Toe by Toe
  8 Green Road
  Baildon
  Shipley BD17 5HL
  Email: info@toe-by-toe.co.uk
  www.toe-by-toe.co.uk

  Tel: 01274 598807
  A Structured Multi-Sensory
  Phonetic Approach to Literacy.

- Winslow Catalogue
  Goyt Side Road
  Chesterfield
  Derbyshire S40 2PH